Aspe

Aspects of Prayer

THE REVEREND JOHN ELEY

The Cooking Canon

Collins
FOUNT PAPERBACKS

William Collins Sons & Co. Ltd

London · Glasgow · Sydney · Auckland

Toronto · Johannesburg

First published in Great Britain in 1990 by Fount Paperbacks

Fount Paperbacks is an imprint of Collins Religious Division,
part of the Collins Publishing Group, 8 Grafton Street,
London W1X 3LA

Copyright © 1990 John Eley

Printed and bound in Great Britain by William
Collins Sons & Co. Ltd, Glasgow

CONDITIONS OF SALE

Contents

Introduction

Prayer, like swimming, can be a life-enhancing experience or it can lead you into the deep waters of the mind and leave you floundering helplessly. Learning to swim and learning how to use swimming for exercise are different things. In a swimming pool there is a basic security, knowing that within reach there are the sides and bottom of the pool and someone to dive in and help you out. There is a boundary to your spirit of adventure: you are limited to swimming in a confined area, no matter how far you try to go each way. This brings a certain security and confidence which is more difficult to maintain whilst swimming in the open sea. If you dive in from a boat it is good to see the hull above you, knowing that it is within easy reach, somewhere you can go for a rest and catch your breath. Remove the boat or lose sight of it, and panic can set in and you can be lost. The boat acts as a form of security whilst still giving you the freedom of the greater waters to exercise and explore.

Many of us who work at prayer probably need this sort of support, which is often given by a local church or house group. There is a danger of limiting the experience of prayer by fearing to move outside the confines or walls of our secure circle, and so not putting the experience and skill to good use, for the

1

greater good as well as the exploration of oneself. However, in other ways a church or group can act as the walls of a swimming pool and keep you locked in within its confines.

This is not the liberating experience that prayer should bring. There is an element of risk in prayer, and it needs to be taken and worked at. There is also a need for a base to which to return to steady oneself, and to examine with others the individual experience, thus strengthening and supporting each other, providing a liberating security and receiving the experience of those who have trodden the same waters before. For some this support may be an individual, a spiritual director, for others a group of close friends.

Like many life skills we need to be shown that there is a relevance for learning them. We need to be supported in the acquiring of new skills and shown that the skill is worth acquiring and practising. If we are not shown the way then how are we to learn? Prayer is one of the less tangible skills, and no examinations can be given to test the student's achievement.

Basic skills and opening doors are best learnt from those who, from their own experience, have found the value and the need of prayer. To bring the basic skills to life there needs to be an awareness of the Being to which we address our prayer. This is sometimes more difficult to comprehend than the physical activities often associated with prayer, such as attending a church service and going through familiar words and rituals. These words and rituals can indeed open our minds and give us insight into

the "generations of minds" that have already
wrestled with words, to explain the incomprehensible
presence and their awareness of the Being to which
their prayer is addressed. These words and rituals
have been wrought from one generation to the next,
from one stage in world history to the next, often
changing so slowly that they have lost the impact
they originally had when used in the time they were
first designed. The way we use these frail words often
reflects the attention we pay to their meaning. To my
mind there is nothing more banal than the corporate
reciting of familiar prayers in church by
congregations who have fallen into the habit of
believing that God is deaf and needs to be addressed
in such a loud voice that the incantations can be
heard outside the stout walls of the building. I would
rather congregations learnt to listen to the words,
familiar as they may be, as they say them. If they can
hear what their neighbour is saying, then the
neighbour is talking too loud – and needs a dig in the
ribs.

However prosaic the public channels of prayer
may seem, they can act as part of the highway that
leads to a deeper understanding of the limitless
possibilities in the voyage of discovery which prayer
can bring, delivering both a freedom and a
responsibility. A freedom in discovering that this
earthly journey is but a part of a greater whole, and a
responsibility in actually finding that our part, no
matter how we undervalue our efforts, has a
relevance and a meaning.

The fatal flaw of arrogance can set in, and we may
feel that we have achieved the heights, only to

discover that we stumble and fall. If you walk through the Lake District there are many times when you will think you have reached the summit of one of the peaks, only to find that there is a little valley before another hill. John Fenton, in one of his lectures on St Luke's Gospel, recalls the experience he had when walking across some narrow parapets at Lincoln Cathedral, with a drop of some eighty feet at each side. His way was protected by highly ornamental stone carving, and yet he felt a little giddy, so he reached out to steady himself, only to feel the firm stone he thought he would find crumbling in his fingers. If we feel that we have arrived at a point of complacent safety in our prayer life, then perhaps the same happens to us. Prayer is also a movement in the stillness, a movement towards God in response to God's movement to us in Jesus Christ. Prayer is the channel provided by God, and from the activity of God through which we are able to address God.

Already I have referred to one person who somewhere along the journey has enhanced my understanding and opened the mind a little on the question of prayer. It is through people and experiences that we come to be aware that the known areas of existence around us are not in our control, but that there are other forces at work and one greater force that controls all the others. There may be in generations to come a new theological language which tries to explain these things, and perhaps we have had a glimpse of it already with the words "May the force be with you", from the ever popular movie *Star Wars*, which could replace the simple

"God Bless" for others.

In the chapters which follow you will find a highly personal journey into prayer which is neither completed nor I hope complicated, as the writer is not a scholar. It is a journey with peaks and valleys of despair, but above all one of optimism and faith influenced by the immediate experiences of an earthly life. I hope the experiences recalled, although often quite unspectacular, will release thoughts and feelings that you too may have, and encourage you to go on searching. But before the search begins in earnest our awareness needs to be aroused.

1

An Awareness of God

Ask a child to draw a picture of God, and you will probably end up with an old man sitting in a large chair on a cloud in the sky looking down upon His creation. Somehow God is seen to be separated from us, and rather like a puppeteer pulling the strings to make everything work. Jewish and Muslim ideas of God tend to separate Him from the world, whereas Christianity combines God's presence and activity in the world with His eternity and infinity, being beyond the world of our experience.

There is some security in this idea of a separation of the immediate presence of God from man, keeping him at a safe distance. The stories of the Fall, with Adam and Eve trying to hide from God, having done precisely the thing they were told not to do, is probably a basic fault in us all. "What the eye does not see the heart cannot grieve over!", is a very old maxim, but it cannot be used with God.

Whenever there was something unexplainable my Father or Mother always replied, "God did it". From an early age I knew that there was something or someone called God, and that He seemed to have most things in his control. This childlike acceptance, that there were some things which we could not explain and indeed could spend lots of time trying to explain without any clear result, was satisfactory enough for a simple faith as a child, and to be quite honest is still fundamental to my belief now.

In those early childhood years it was accepted that everyone knew about God. Someone was telling you, but no one ever checked everything was accepted, when the truth was that in the main you had to make the discovery for yourself.

A slow and limiting process this may have been, but as the years pass perhaps it has left a wider vision than that confined to the Church. I am still not convinced that an early attendance at Sunday School would have done an awful lot for my faith, other than revealing, in a childlike way, the stories of God and His activities in dealing with humanity in the Old and New Testaments. Probably like many others I may well have left the Church at more formative years, and like many other gone back to it in old age without having increased my understanding of God, and still having the childlike ideas to work on. These ideas would bring back not only memories of childhood and security, but a feeling of being close to parents, and those secure days when as a child you did not have to make decisions.

The very idea that you could have a personal relationship with God did not even enter into the discussions in those days. As in the relationship between father and son, which is the model often used, there was still the possibility of a distance. You asked your Father for something and he said yes or no. When the answer was no, so another gap was put in between you, a little more distance. As we grow older and more independent, so the relationship, although in many ways close, becomes different, and you no longer rely on what your parents say and do as being the measure by which you live, and you make your own decisions. It is obvious that the childhood understanding of God closely linked with that of your parents, and your growth away from them, is also influenced. As we grow we become stronger and more independent, and so we feel we do not need to rely on parents, so why rely on God? It is very difficult to keep a concept of a providing God and a God whom we should address, when the earthly distances become so great, the usual gaps between parent and child.

There is no doubt that the experiences of childhood play a strong part in our understanding and perceptions of God. In my own life it was not until I went to primary school that the person of Jesus came to the fore. Up till then anything that happened or could not be explained was attributed to God. I was too young to ask who this God person was, but living close to nature, the rotation of agriculture and the change of the seasons, the births and deaths of animals, all these mysteries were attributed to God. Indeed we did plough the fields and scatter the corn, but it seemed to me that it was another mystery that made the corn grow, and this power was God. So from an early age God was seen to be the energy or force by which everything had life. It was very easy to accept because the question ''Why?'' became too big to ask or comprehend.

My early education did nothing to help me ask questions. It was very much a read, mark and learn situation, there was no room for the questions ''Why?'' or ''How?'' Everything was done in a matter of fact way. We were filled with facts. Even the injection of a little religion was a question of accepting everything as fact, and even when that education did take place it was done before the main timetable of the school day began, outside the main course of things. The Vicar came at a certain time before school began. In this way it is easy to see how we continued or began to learn that the way people dealt with the things of God was "outside" the everyday norm, outside the routine and stride of life, sectioned off and kept at a safe distance. Secondary school was very similar, although we did have Religious Education on the timetable, but we always saw these lessons as a bit of a break from the routine and not to be taken too seriously. They were a respite from the urgency of the norm and really had little relevance. Indeed, after the second or third year the top two streams did not have Religious Education, and in more recent years it has been watered down more to "Life Skills" or at best some form of social activity. The edge on God has gone off. It was never the main topic of conversation in the playground, as you can imagine.

A little relevance was brought to God and life by a clergyman who came to the school to teach us some of the skills in English and Drama. It was a new experience to have in the classroom a man with a dog collar, teaching us something about a subject other than the one we thought he knew most about. He was firm, fair and kind, and he certainly was not hiding his light under a bushel. We could all see he was a God person. His wife too taught at the school, and neither of them used their time with us to push religion at us. They got on with their jobs and did them well. For the first time I had seen that God's activities did, as I suspected, extend beyond the things we could not answer.

The person of Jesus is the most striking action of God being seen in some dramatic way to have intervened in human affairs. It is an event which has cut a slash across world history and cannot easily be ignored. "God became man and dwelt among us."

I am in danger of trying to become too theological if I try to explain what the arrival of Jesus meant, when I am trying to raise from my own experience how I have come to understand the presence of God. People, as I say time and again, play a very important part and in often very strange ways. My brother was not happy at school, and he used to work himself up into quite a state over school work and activities connected with education. He was not an unintelligent lad, and I now believe that his real frustration was that the method of learning that he had to use was too limiting, and the experiences of his pre-school life opened his mind more than the subsequent education was to allow. I saw his pain and unhappiness about school, and resolved that it would not be the same for me. I would read, mark, learn and conform, but not necessarily accept. If 2 + 2 made 4 that I could accept willingly. If b + b = c and the teacher said that was the correct answer, then I would accept it, although I did not understand it and would not ask the question "Why?" as it would probably open up areas that I could not comprehend. Education filled my mind, but did not open it to learning; that was the system in those days.

Fortunately my experiences before school had helped me realize that there would always be things in life we did not understand, and that these were all part of God's creation. What I had to learn was the relevance of everything we do in connection with God and communing with Him.

Like so many others, I left school and set about earning a living, still keeping in touch loosely with the Church, and it was not until my return to Suffolk that I began to study seriously the religion I had naturally taken on. Exciting and fervent times! Exciting because I was able to expand my knowledge of the Christian faith, and I wanted to. To my first old Testament teacher, Muriel Powell, I owe a great debt of gratitude. Our sympathies were of a similar nature: the love of the Old Testament, and the actions of God reported by those who wrote and believed by the people of the times in the Hebrew nations. It seemed very simple. The King was somehow chosen by God and reflected His will to the people. If the King or the people did something wrong then they were punished and brought back into line. It all seemed so simple, yet when you looked closer it was not the case, but the golden thread which runs through the Old Testament is a God who cares for His people and wants them for Himself. The steadfast love that God has written for His creation is reflected in all that is written in the Bible. This idea of God's steadfast love, one which could never run out, and which despite all mankind's failings was always there, is what has fired me ever since. It is not a thin veneer of sincerity but a solid trunk of reality. We seem called to reflect that in the world, in all that we do and say and are.

When it comes to praying then it has not been difficult for my prayers to be addressed directly to God. Indeed, the Lord's prayer immediately directs our address to God: "Our Father..." We address Him personally and directly, and this every human being has the right to do. Separated though we are from the early experiences of Jesus's disciples by time, experience and the writings of many ages, we are not separated from God. It is He who has given us the spark of life, and we are all of equal worth in His sight, we are made in His image. We separate ourselves from God by choosing not to pay attention to Him, in not thanking Him and seeking to learn more about His action in our lives.

In our human frailty or vanity we let other things take over and make them our gods. Things get out of proportion. The need to survive in this life often pushes out any thought of paying attention to that part of us that will see us into eternity, if indeed we have even considered such a concept. There is an immense difficulty in seeing a relevance to anything that does not affect the reality that we experience in the present, and so we pay infinite attention to all those things which affect our immediate experience. We need to be able to extend this to see that the relevant things of today can be influenced by the way we approach the prospect of being with God in heaven.

For the poor, as is often the case, the hope of the world to come and the immediate presence of God is far better than their present reality. This has led to the wide belief that it is easier for the poor to enter the Kingdom of Heaven than for the rich! This is a form of humbug I cannot really accept. Indeed, we who have plenty need to learn that we are all poor. All the things that we possess in this life are indeed lent to us. We may own things in this life, and indeed have great wealth and achievement, but in fact we possess nothing, for everything belongs to God. Even the body in which we live and move and have our being will one day cease to exist, and that spark of life which is ourselves has a chance of returning to God.

The awful truth is that we have a responsibility to do something about it, to see that we do find our way back to God. Not that He needs to find His way to us, as we are His, but we have been given a free will, a gift only He could make. It is a free will to try to live our lives for the improvement of ourselves and others. It would seem that God does not want us as slaves but as free people, living for His praise and glory. For what reason we will have to wait and see. If we become separated from that quest then our lives become less relevant and we lose a sense of purpose and a hope which can give a meaning, a fullness to life.

There is a paradox. If we seek a freedom from God and ignore Him, and try to live a life wholly dedicated to fulfilment in this world, then we become ensnared in the things of this world. We lose a dimension which in difficult times can give us hope, and in successful times bring a humility that keeps us free from believing that the success is our own doing, rather than our collaboration of talents with others and God in order to glorify Him. We are all part of a greater energy which as a whole is the creative activity of God. The universe is for ever changing, there are deaths and new lives every minute of the day and night. These miracles we so easily take for granted. So-called human achievement loses that element which acknowledges the creative activity of God, and man pats himself on the back instead of saying "by the grace of God". Congratulations flow on our achievements – a new job, an engagement, a marriage, a new child, success at work, promotion, so on and so forth – and it is right to be joyful on these occasions. Man makes great strides into space, and a new medical cure is found, a new work of art is born and praises are lavished, and it is right to celebrate. For most of us our successes are not so spectacular or noticeable as a successful cake or a well made dress. A good crop of vegetables from the garden or the painting job completed well, passing the driving test or simply surviving another day with a smile are all achievements for which we need to thank God, yet so often we let the opportunity slip, and the more we let it slip the less relevant it becomes and we begin to believe too much in our own abilities and try to walk without Him. "Ah, yes", I hear you say, "but there are many successful people who do not seem to acknowledge the presence of God in their activities, and why do so many bad people seem to prosper?" I would only answer that the true prosperity we seek is not here in this world, important though it may seem, but is indeed in finding our way to be with God in heaven. We seek a prosperity-plus and we can choose to seek that or not.

It is when things go wrong, sometimes very

seriously wrong, that we see as our only hope some form of divine intervention, and so we turn our attention to God to ask for help. Please do not think that just because I venture to write this book I am not doing or have not done the same things myself. The real sadness is that we have been aware, somewhere within us, of the presence of God, locked away in some drawer of the mind, and we only bring it out when there is an apparent need of some intervention that, we hope, will put things to rights. I wish to rob no one of this hope. From time to time we all are brought up sharp by circumstance which bring into clear focus our need of God. From the moment it happens there is cause for some joy because we have at least found that need once again. We cannot escape it, as we are part of His creative activity and God suffers with us. The great loss is if we do not realize or find that hope, and in that hope the freedom to place our cares in God while still finding the strength to work through the difficulties in which we may be ensnared.

Our problem seems to be how to find God and His relevance in all that we experience in seeing, hearing and living in the life around us. For me all that we experience presents an aspect of God and His creative activity. We can also look at the achievements of man and nature. But when things to apparently wrong, when good people suffer and the innocent are hurt, where is the action of God in this? Natural disasters are the worst to try and explain, if indeed there is any explanation. In many disasters where man is involved there is in part an explanation – the terrorist's bomb, the incompetent workman, the human error – but what of the Divine error? It would seem that earthquakes and the like fall into these categories, and any explanations or rationalizations tread on thin ice. We see these things through our limited sight and vision as mankind, and cannot seek to give a satisfactory answer. Suffering and pain have no easy answer, no matter how hard we try to find one. Through the eyes of faith and with hope in a loving God, that suffering can perhaps, by the power of that same God, be turned into some form of redemption for those who suffer and die.

Death is that door through which we must all pass if we are to come into the presence of God at its deepest level. We all have to face it, and for many the death of a loved one may be the trigger by which we start thinking again about God. Why does a loving God demand that a person, the person whom we love, must die and leave us? Once again we are limiting the activity of God to our own immediate experience. On the death of a loved one we experience a pain and a grief that is like no other: an emptiness, an anger, a frustration, a loneliness which is unequalled. We all know it must happen, and more often than not we put it out of our minds, or at least push it into one of those little drawers until it is pillaged by the thief of life itself. Our twentieth-century attitude to death in the Western world is in the main an unhealthy one. The event itself has become sterilized, and we are protected from it by medical and other supportive care. Life has to go on, we have little time to care for those who are dying, so we try to buy protection from the fact by calling in the supportive agencies to help us cope with the needs of the dying person. All too often we leave it too late to help the dying person to let go. We avoid talking about the fact, or sharing together the preparations for what has to be done afterwards; we push it to one side as if to protect ourselves. Death takes place wherever possible outside the home, and when it does happen we are still expected, in England at least, to have a stiff upper lip. None of these things protects us from the awful pain of the reality.

There are those, though, who do have the courage to share with those they love their thoughts about dying, and there are others who will share in caring for the dying person, and there are those who have the privilege of dying at home. For others it is so sudden that preparation cannot be made. We need to use death as a focus for life. It can also help us focus on our hope for the future. The way we each prepare for death, if we have any faith, can help others.

Even death itself needs to be seen as part of the creative activity of a loving God. In old age, or where there is desperate suffering through illness and many kinds of disability, this is easier to accept. When the person is a child or young with ''a full life ahead of them'', then our judgement is clouded and we naturally feel more anger. There are no easy answers, and yet we all live within seconds of the event. There remains a mystery and we have to live with these questions. It is part of the quest of life itself.

The business of life so easily detracts from our Creator. Wrapped up as we are in furthering our own existence, from time to time we must find release from utter dependence upon mankind, which so often leads to our being let down. Sparing time to approach some of the larger questions, and the quest for an understanding of God can bring some perspective to our turmoil and some meaning. This does not mean that we achieve Faith itself, but a thought on the journey means that we are on the way and we must realize that faith will not bring knowledge but perhaps a little understanding.

For me God reveals Himself in all the creative activity that goes on around us, in His creation and in our fellow human beings. We have deeper insights from time to time which encourage us in this quest. What we are working towards remains a mystery, but we can make the path better for others by the way we lead our lives, and by being strengthened in the challenges that we face if we ask Him for help. The answers may not come clearly through some celestial megaphone, as we would so often wish, but perhaps they are slowly revealed and confirmed as we tread the perilous path of faith through prayer.

It is in this journey that we find a freedom to cope with this world, and learn to use the talents that we have been given to enhance it and share in the creative love that God has. Our search for God so often begins with the Bible, to see how others have understood His ways. We must not lose sight of those who over the centuries have added to this quest with their thoughts and writings, including those who write and speak to us today. We seek to hear through them the voice of God. The old saying, "A prophet is not without honour except in his own kingdom" speaks to us still. We look back into the past centuries, to the writers and thinkers of ages long ago whose works have stayed the course, writing from another time and yet still speaking to us today. Yet we must not lose sight of the prophet of our time through whom God also speaks to us.

It takes a bold man to say today that he is a prophet, and perhaps that is for others to decide. But while people are still prepared to make sacrifices to quest after God, then we have hope for mankind.

For my own part, I am one of those who struggle with the concepts of God presented to us in the written word, and I seek to see more of Him revealed in the people and the world around us. One bishop I worked for called me an optimist, but I like to think of myself as a realist whose quest is incomplete. Mother Julian of Norwich sums up my belief in God in her meditation on an acorn. She looked at it, saw its smallness, and contemplated that into which it would grow, saying that, ''All things will be well, all manner of things will be well''.

2

This Person called Jesus

The person of Jesus appeared later in my life, after I had begun to believe in God the Creator of the Universe. We had heard at Christmas about the Son of God, but we were still thanking God for Him and so it was to God that we looked. Why we thanked God for Him began to unfold as the years went by, and a mature understanding began to develop as life took its toll. It was Jesus who made real prayer possible and relevant. His humanity unlocked the door that trapped us in this earthly kingdom and made possible entry into heaven.

I have been blessed in not suffering the Sunday School image of Jesus born in a stable, always looking terribly sweet and holy in later life. The pious pictures which bless many schools and Sunday Schools were not a part of my upbringing. In fact I never went to Sunday School, and the Village School itself was void of any real colour, saving for the Holman Hunt picture of Christ with the Lamp knocking on the wooden door. The meaning of the picture was never explained to us, and it hung there, unexplained, for most of my schooling. In fact images of Christ have never really played an important part in my spirituality, although I can understand that some people can help their prayer and meditation by focusing on a Crucifix or Icon.

Most churches in my native Suffolk had a plain cross with no figure, once explained to me as a symbol of the empty cross, showing that Christ rose from the dead.

The question of Christ's resurrection has never been a difficult one for me to accept. Living in the country, and with a childhood surrounded by God's miracles as they appear in nature, I simply accept that if that is what God wanted to do then He would do it. And so He did: Christ rose from the dead. As a child it did not seem a spectacular event to me, after all, things were dying around us all the time and there was always new life in the spring. Some animals survived, others died and new ones were born, it was all part of a cycle and we human beings were a part of it too. It was and remains for me all part of the ongoing of life, and that is that.

Perhaps I was blessed with my upbringing and uncomplicated ability to accept things as they were explained to me without question. I suppose a lot of things depend on how you are told, and whether or not you think that it is really necessary to know the actual way things work. I really cannot remember how Jesus was introduced to me, but guess it was through the priest regularly visiting us at school. He would sway from near the hot stove, talking to us, in a very slow voice, about the things of Jesus. Then this experience was enhanced by the preparations for Christmas, during which I was far more interested in all the preparations in the kitchen than in the church. But at least I did learn that Jesus was born rather mysteriously, his mother was a Virgin, and Joseph, his Father, was a carpenter. That they were on their way to pay their taxes and to be counted, when Mary's time came, and Jesus was born in a stable, because the Inn was full. It all seemed perfectly logical to me and, without any of the romanticism of the years, it is a story I can accept.

To add colour to the event we have the stories of the Star, with the Shepherds having a nudge from a passing flight of Angels, to go and see this thing that had happened; and the Wise Men, who were always looking for a sign about something, spotted a new star and decided to follow it until they stumbled across the crowded stable with Mary, Joseph, the Shepherds, a few cattle and there, in the manger, the Baby Jesus. The gospels really tell us very little, but then their writers were not present at the events they record. What I would like to know is, what about the Inn-keeper's wife and other people at the Inn? No matter where or when a baby is born, it always seems to be treated as good news, and everyone, yes everyone, wants to hold the baby, and I am sure that even the Baby Jesus made His presence felt with a healthy pair of lungs. So, yes, we have sugared the pill, or at least the story-tellers have. After all, just another baby would hardly make the headlines today let alone in Palestine centuries ago.

We tend to lose sight of the figure of Jesus unless we read St Luke's Gospel, with brave attempts at linking together pious stories about his childhood and appearance in the Temple. But there is very little there about the person who suddenly and dramatically appears, following John the Baptist, who was already preaching a Gospel of repentance when Jesus comes to him to be baptized. We have no

physical description of Jesus, his face, eyes, nose,
mouth and whether or not he was bearded. Artists
have done their best, and so we have the Christ of a
Thousand Faces. But is it really necessary to have a
"picture" of the Christ figure? I believe it is not, and
in many ways we are blessed by not having a
description. To have a description of Christ in the
physical sense limits the appeal. If we are made, as I
believe we are, in the image of God, and we know
that God has many faces, then it is best not to limit
the picture of the physical Jesus, for there is a little
bit of God in all of us and therefore a little bit of
Jesus. So there is no need to focus upon a physical
picture of Jesus and believe that is exactly how He
looked. It does not matter.

We seem to know so little about those first thirty
years of His life, and all we do know about Him does
not come from the Bible. An elderly church organist
once told me a story which is reputed to come from
the Koran. There were a crowd of people gathered
around a dead dog. One of the crowd said, "Look at
his scars, he must have been a fighter", another said,
"Look how thin he was, he must have been a
scavenger", and another voice said, "Yes, but look
at his teeth, they are as white as pearls." The others
looked around to see who had said this but the man
was passing on down the road. Another said, "Oh,
that must have been Jesus. He sees some good in
everything." Whether or not I have worded the story
accurately enough is not the point, what it does show
is a little about Jesus. They do not see Jesus exactly
as He is, walking on down the street, but they
remember what sort of person He is, someone who

looks for the good. So we have an aspect of Jesus from outside the Bible, and another source, a snippet that tells us something about Him.

There were lots of these snippets and experiences of Jesus that the gospel writers came across, especially St Mark, who is generally believed to be the first of the gospel writers. His gospel story moves on apace, with lots of "Press Cutting" type incidents in Jesus's life, each one revealing something about this man Jesus. Mark is anxious to get on with the story, and so we are soon transported through the promise of the Old Testament about a "Voice crying in the wilderness" to the appearance of John the Baptist, and the arrival of Jesus from Nazareth. Then there is the Baptism, and then Jesus is sent off to the wilderness to be tempted by Satan, accompanied by a few Angels just to look after Him. This is followed by a quick two-liner about John's arrest and the beginning of Jesus's ministry: "The time is fulfilled, and the kingdom of God is at hand; repent, and believe the Gospel." Jesus's ministry has begun.

St Mark continues at this pace, adding five blocks of stories of Jesus's teaching before going into the Passion Narrative. Mark has punctuated his gospel with pithy sayings from Jesus and the occasional miracle, just to push the point home that this is someone special. But there is no description of Him as such. We learn so much about Him by what He says and does, not by the way He looks. In fact the physical side of Jesus would not have helped one blind beggar, dear Bartimaeus, who had heard about Jesus and called out to Him for help. I always like

Bartimaeus. He had the courage to ask for help and he called out, and by all accounts he was helped. The important thing to remember is that he did not see Jesus, but had heard about Him and called to Him. That is what we call prayer. He had the hope, the faith even, that if he sincerely called out to Jesus He would help him. Once healed Bartimaeus did not just give up on Jesus. Mark reports that he "followed Him in the way", he followed the life of Jesus as best he could, but knew he could always call out to Him when he needed some help. This some would say is prayer too.

The physical person of Jesus is not made known to us today. Quite frankly we do not need to know what he looked like. What we need to come to understand is the essence of what He was trying to get at. In lots of ways I would find it a hindrance if I had to picture Jesus in my mind as I prayed. In fact I do not have that problem, although for some such a picture helps. My upbringing has meant that I have an awareness of God, and really Jesus came along afterwards to show us the way to approach and address God, and to work towards a godly life when we are here on earth, preparing ourselves for a stab at the Kingdom of Heaven. In fact I believe that the Lord's Prayer, as it has become known, has a great deal to offer, explaining to us what we are about when we try to lead the Christian life.

Our Father in heaven... addresses the fact that the Lord and Creator of us all is over all, in all and of all, but is above everything a Father we can address and learn more of.

Hallowed be thy name... Holy, magnificent and

very special is this Father in Heaven. God whom we call upon is Holy and special.

Thy will be done... an endless prayer for me. In all things, whether it is just before I go on Television to cook, or having ladened the celestial ear with a long list of petitions, I end my prayers with this "Thy will be done". It acknowledges the fact that it is God's will that we must seek, and no matter how we want or need or feel that others want or need certain answers to prayer, the answers that we receive may not be what we would desire, and often the answer is difficult to perceive, so it is always "Thy will be done..."

On earth as it is in Heaven... a pious hope, or is this linking the earthly world and the divine into a whole? For the God whom we address is Lord of all, those things that are seen and experienced in this world, and those things which are not seen and not experienced and often subject to speculation. So we wish the will of God to be done in the earthly and the Divine. Our difficulty is discerning that will, and the way we discern it is to try to identify with Him, from what we know of Him in Jesus and what we experience in our lives. The revelation of God's will has not ended at the empty tomb. What we need to do today is to be able to discern God's will in a modern world, and being able to address ourselves to prayer enhances our reception of the continuing revelation of God.

Give us this day our daily bread... both literally and spiritually. Is this a request for food, or is it for some spiritual enlightenment? Remembering the words that "man cannot live by bread alone" we are left to wonder. I like to think that it is a little bit of both. Remembering the old maxim that an army marches on its stomach – and I always found that as a student if you were well fed you studied better – perhaps, apart from the disciplines of Lent, it is a request for both food and spiritual enlightenment, and there is no shame in requesting either.

Forgive us our sins as we forgive those who sin against us... The prayer leads us on to more sensitive areas where we have to face some of the real battles against good and evil. As we ask to be forgiven our sins, so we acknowledge that we are indeed sinners and need to be forgiven. Is the measure of the forgiveness we receive similar to that which we give others? How do we totally forgive others when the hurt is often deep and real, and we have to be prepared to forgive fully as well as to repent fully. Deep matters, which I will go into elsewhere, but we do have to face the awful fact that we are indeed sinners and that we need to repent. An instantaneous feeling of relief and foregiveness is not my experience, but God gives us this anyway and freely.

Lead us not into temptation... well, let's all be honest: we are all tempted from time to time. It need not be the dramatic temptation of Jesus in the Wilderness, but those silly, simple things that seem to crop up every day in life. "I'm sure the firm will not miss one stamp", "I really did only have one cream cake." Well, I am sure temptation like that comes to us all regularly, but then there are those temptations to try to live without God. True we have the free choice, because that is what makes us human beings so different from other creatures. To turn our back on God is often a temptation, to pretend that there is no other force or being other than ourselves. Many intellectuals, scientists and thinkers put up good arguments for the non-existence of a creative activity which we call God. I hope it really is simply a question of language, and they may well be suffering from some basic and bad Sunday School teaching. Scientists and many great thinkers do not like living with questions, and they do like knowledge. Faith is not knowledge, neither is it a pious hope.

Deliver us from evil... an acknowledgement that there are evil things, bad things, in this world, which Jesus Himself was aware of. I think we often like to put the idea of evil out of our minds, and when we do it seems that is when the evil part of our lives can begin to take over. We need daily to ask for deliverance from evil, from all that is bad, and to seek courage to ask for help in fighting the same.

So the Lord's Prayer, as well as the gospels and all the writings in the New Testament, can lay claim to telling us something about Jesus, but it is not the whole picture. We have to remember that in Jesus God was revealed in human form at a time when people were receptive, and that revelation did not end with the ascension of Jesus into heaven. Indeed, through His Church we have a key to discern the continuing revelation of the mind of Christ. In our human frailty, though, we have somewhat clouded the picture and often got our lines crossed, so that the disunited picture of the Church fogs the picture of Jesus. We are in danger of lifting our thoughts above the reality of the Jesus person.

Often we are looking for more than what there is, and not seeing what actually is there. Without doubt Jesus was rather good at upsetting the powers-that-be of His time. He spoke of Love and Forgiveness which were freely given, and that there was no need for any sacrifice other than the life that we have to be lived in His name. When things go well, thank Him; when things go wrong, ask Him for help. But above all we need to have a Faith in Him, because he experienced our human lot and was able to open the door of heaven for us all. It is through Jesus, God's Son – who by whatever means came to live in this life as a mortal human being by dying and being risen from the dead — that the door to glory is opened for us all. It really is not a complicated message, but then Truth is never complicated. What has made it all so complicated has been the questioning minds through the ages, minds of those who have been seen to be great and influential, and yet who have forgotten the blind faith of the poor.

3

The Places People Pray

The weekly round of the Sunday visit to a church can give the impression that this is where we do it, this is where we go to pray. In part the truth is there, but if we stay with that we limit prayer itself. Yes, for many it is important to have a place to withdraw to and pray, but we do not need to limit the activity of prayer until we are there. The social aspect of going to church is a strong one, and the benefits are enormous, but do we actually make preparation before we go, or do we simply depend upon the atmosphere and activity of the place to help us tune into God? The activity of a church service can border on the entertaining and reassuringly familiar, and can block the way to prayer.

As human beings we have a natural desire to withdraw sometimes to small, comfortable and familiar places that help us feel secure, when often the world around us is not. It is like retreating to the womb, that place of utmost security. How many people in modern homes long for a little corner where they can be alone, and a place they can call their own, where they will not be observed? For some, the need is to experience a kind of otherness and an awareness of God, for others, it is just for a little peace.

The range of places in which I have been called to

lead public prayer has been enormous, from the humble village church to the cavernous cathedral. Each has its role and emphasis when it comes to prayer. In the country village church on a Sunday there may be few people, and yet the building will have an atmosphere which is unique, where for hundreds of years people have come together to pray. You add your prayers to a chain of intercession offered from this place, which has become "Holy Ground". Your presence joins the presence of those who have gone before, thus building upon the history of that place. All too often the feelings of warmth and security that a church can bring reflect memories of childhood days, when we were taken to church by parents trying to do the right thing. These memories flood back to the innocence of childhood before we were marred by the world.

The design of the village church and the appendages it has gathered over the years sometimes detract from its original simplicity. Rood screens and pews have detracted from the sense of space and openness that was often intended. Gradually space has given way to the monumental. The original intention was simply a space where you could go to pray, and in an uncluttered way find time with God. There must be very few village churches today which have escaped the litter of the ages in the way of furnishing and other additions.

Patrons and worthies of every kind, and with every good intention, have adorned the churches to the Glory of God and their own eternal memory. Windows that once opened onto the world and let us view it from within the church were filled and put to good use, with parables and biblical stories told in glass, which in their turn, it is argued, helped educate those who could not read. Pictures and carvings of saints remind us of the great multitude than no man can number, who have prayed and who were leaders in their worlds. All these wonderful adornments fill some of the most simple of churches.

As styles developed so the architecture became more ornate, and the carvings were incorporated in the architecture, and it became the norm to fill the churches with this sort of "busy-ness" that detracts from peace and tranquillity, speaking rather of continual movement and leaving nothing peaceful for the eye to rest on. It would seem that the early buildings were bare and simple, and over the years we have decorated them overmuch.

The building and decoration of our larger parish churches and cathedrals reflect the histories of their age. A town probably reflected a more wealthy community than a village or hamlet, which unless blessed with a "wealthy patron" probably had a very simple building to worship in. Human nature demands that where there is wealth, at times it is not a bad thing to show it, though in a tasteful way. With every good intention traders, lords temporal and spiritual, where they had wealth, ploughed their resources into buildings which spoke of the might and majesty of God and of the success of their age.

I ask the question, "What were the thoughts of the poor and often illiterate who saw these buildings go up in the name of the God whom they were to worship?" We have little or no record. The greatness of these buildings does indeed instill a sense of awe and wonder, an appreciation of the talents which God has given man, and how he has used them to reflect God's glory, but do they provide us with places of prayer?

Cathedrals more than large parish churches provide us with a chance to be anonymous while attending an act of public worship and prayer. You can nip in and out of the daily cathedral evensong, and it is unlikely that you will be bothered by anyone. The sheer size of some of these buildings means that you can see someone coming and usually escape with a little dignified speed! The worship offered is usually led by the clergy and choir, all that is needed is your presence and mind. There is little need to utter a word, and you can simply be carried into a form of meditation by the skilful musicianship and mastery of the language by those employed to do the job. In this way you can withdraw into that small corner of worship and prayer which you can call your own. Being alone in a crowd then takes on a whole new meaning. Should the aspirations of the visiting choir and clergy fall short of their ability, and your meditation is interrupted, then the building and its adornments can come to the rescue, and, while some village choir wrestles with the *Cantate Domino*, you can cast an eye over a window, picture or carving and slip into your small world that way. I tend to think that those large buildings which have not been adorned too much by additions and, seen in the way in which they were designed, even if they are ornate, tend to be less of a distraction. The most successful ones of modern times must surely be the Anglican Cathedral in Liverpool which, although modestly ornate, has not as yet gathered the clutter of generations of benefactors wishing to raise monuments to various personages and causes. How wonderful it would be to see Westminster Abbey stripped of the clutter of the ages, and, viewed as the original architects perceived it, it might be a stronger aid to prayer and a more restful place.

Mercifully, most of these large churches which, in order to survive, have given themselves over to the tourist industry, do offer small corners where you can nip in for some peace and quiet. In Westminster Abbey there is St Edward's Chapel, which is really an oasis in the heart of London. The peace is unique above the noise of the Abbey, which really hits you when you come out into the main body of the church.

The quest for silence may not be one pursued by many simply because it is something so few have experienced, a real silence without noise, other than that of your own breathing. In towns and cities, and indeed in many villages, there is the all-penetrating noise of the internal combustion engine, either on the road or flying precariously overhead. It is almost impossible to find that cell of silence which can rest the hearing part of the brain. In recent years I have been discussing the building of a new church, and one of the features I requested from the architect was that we should include a sound-proofed room, really sound-proof, where we could experience silence. It was pleasing to have so much agreement from those who were discussing the ideas with me. We had discovered that, out of all the churches in the town, there was not one where you could be absolutely still and free from noise. We agreed too that silence contributed to the prayerful presence in a building.

The parish church can be the welcoming heart of a community, and on a Sunday morning the Family Eucharist can take on many forms. To try to educate a congregation to silence is not easy, and with children running around the place the priest has to use other skills to equip himself to survive and help the congregation. Many churches provide crèches, but still families rightly wish to have their little ones with them for all or part of the service. There is no doubt that if the leader of the worship becomes irritated, then the fever spreads throughout the congregation.

Major festivals such as Christmas and Easter bring many to the holy places who otherwise may not darken their doors until the next festival, unless interrupted in their interregnum by a wedding, baptism or funeral. Coming to the holy place is important for them, even if perhaps not understanding all that goes on. In one of my parishes we introduced a candlelight carol service, and many attended who had not been for some years. The following year I was continually being accosted by non-church goers asking, "We are going to have our candle service again this year, aren't we vicar?"

I always enjoy the major festivals of the church, not so much for the large congregations but for those moments after they have gone when their presence is still in the building lingering, not wanting to leave.

To experience what I mean you need to be at the Christmas Midnight Eucharist and the Christmas Day morning services, and then attend the evensong at night... which is said, and to which no one ever comes! You don't really need to say the Office, but you can feel the presence of all those who have come to this holy place and have offered up prayers and thanksgivings. Perhaps their souls are lingering on, having a little holiday all of their own in this holy place, while that mortal part attends to the more physical pleasures of the festival.

In a strange way having the number of people passing through begins to add to the credibility of a holy place. A church that is prayed in lives. It becomes attractive to others and holiness rubs off on those who visit.

There are other holy places which offer gateways into prayer. Religious communities are power houses of prayer and offer an oasis or retreat and worship that we find refreshing. The daily routine of attention to prayer strengthens and gives credibility to the whole house. Here many people will come to draw upon this well of resourcefulness in prayer, recharging their batteries for the life that they lead. Quite often I have discovered that the spirituality offered at such places is not really in tune with their own, and I have found that difficult. The fact that they do exist and give a holy place to help prayer can often be used in your own way.

Holy places of pilgrimage were rife in medieval times, and pilgrims came from near and far to ask for the favours of the saints, both for cure of body and soul. In England today there are those who run shrines of various kinds where the faithful come to pray. Walsingham in Norfolk is a prayerful watering hole for those seeking refreshment and sometimes healing. At Cleator Moor in Cumbria there is a Roman Catholic Shrine to which pilgrims tread annually, providing another wishing well of prayer in which to dip, and they faithfully return year after year.

I am blessed, as I have stated earlier, that in my childhood years I was never brought up to think that the only place to pray was the church building itself. If nothing else I owe this to the school assemblies each morning and the priest who took me for confirmation, simply opening the idea of saying prayers morning and night. However, as a youngster there was a need within me to make a holy place. This need was eventually fulfilled in the conversion of the old shepherd's hut at the bottom of the garden – often used as a chicken shed, coal house and a general play area – into a chapel. There was a plain wooden cross and a couple of jam jars that became flower vases. How long this holy place survived I do not know, but it did have one thing in common with holy places of the Old Testament: it was on the top of a hill.

Moses went up to Mount Sinai to receive the Ten Commandments, Jesus preached on a mountainside and went "up" to pray, so my little chapel or holy place at the bottom of the garden, but on the top of a hill, was all right by me. In the first home I had in Suffolk I had the luxury of a small room I called the study, and this was often where I used to pray, and, sometimes joined by a friend, said compline. This was the place and this was where we prayed; although it was not a church building as such it did provide the place.

The pressure points in life often lead us to retreat to some place of prayer. Hospitals are not always blessed with chapels in the early stage of their development, but those which are provide a place of refuge for those who need them. In the hospital where I worked we had a chapel included in the building of the new unit. It was simply a room, which some would say could have been put to better use. However, it was used, and often, by many people, staff and patients alike. It provided a refuge and place for searching; it was indeed a holy place.

When I became a priest and was called to celebrate communion at one of the local hospitals, as a relief for the chaplain, the somewhat prayerful atmosphere was "enhanced" in the vestry at least by six shrouded corpses which were resting there before being taken to the mortuary when the next portering team came on duty. This early morning reminder of one's own mortality first thing on a Sunday can help to heighten one's desire to pray for the dead.

Going back to the hilltop theory, the idea of withdrawing to a high place for prayer rests with us even in the twentieth century. Whoever decided the placing of Guildford Cathedral must have shared a similar spirituality to those who placed the magnificent Lincoln Cathedral where it is, although the latter has a plateau to the north, whereas Guildford is somewhat isolated. We go up to the Holy Place on Top of the Hill to pray, and so we did as faithful Christians on Bank Holiday Mondays, at the whim of the bishop, walking from miles around. Glastonbury Tor is a reminder of others who have seen it was a good thing to go up a hill to pray, although some say this did not start off as a holy place.

Walking in the hills and finding isolation in the Lake District can help in the finding of a place to pray, but it is fairly obvious that these places are aids to prayer and not an excuse for prayer. It is argued that a church building is indeed a living prayer, and reflects the seriousness with which the community takes to God. I would suggest that the greater challenge is to let go of the building and seek more deeply. However, to remove them altogether may not help others to find a way, but they do act as pointers.

There is, I suppose, a sort of puritanical streak about me. Amidst the busy-ness of life I long for a simplicity and purity which has been long since lost. Yes, I am moved by the glories of our architectural and artistic heritage, and the great buildings do instill a sense of awe and wonder. It would be too cynical to believe that every person who dedicated their lives to these buildings were doing so not for any glory of their own but to the glory of that creative activity from which they gained their skills and insights, but it just might have played the tiniest part in it and we should allow them a little vanity.

If some buildings have lost their innocence through the adjuncts of owners and centuries we are not to blame the architects for the present results. There were those who had positive battles with forces other than their own when things went wrong, as at Ely when the central tower collapsed and they built that magnficent octagon instead. Perhaps too we should not accuse them of vainglory, since who

would have seen Ely when it was first completed? –
only a few townsfolk and pilgrims who stumbled
upon this glorious remote pile. Perhaps cathedrals
should be viewed from the air, as their towers point
to heaven. So heaven looks down on them in the
medieval mind, and it knows that this is where holy
people are. The humble village church says as much
too.

So why do we have this desire for a place, a spot,
an area, a hole where we can pray or find prayer?
What is it that motivates us and yet, when we find
the place, often leaves us unsatisfied? How many
Abbots, Bishops and Architects of old died before
their dreams became reality? And why is it that
succeeding generations have deemed that what they
built was not enough, and so have adapted and
played around with these centres of holiness, burying
even deeper the simplicity with which many spoke?

It would seem that no matter how hard we try,
how many designs we perfect and offer, how many
buildings or places we achieve, we are never going to
find fulfilment in one particular place. Our search
then speaks of a deeper need and sense in finding the
reality of our spritual roots. For a time a place or
church fulfils a need for us as individuals. There are
those to which we will wish to return from time to
time, to top up, because we feel they are holy places,
where we feel in communion with that otherness.
However, we cannot all our lives have that mobility
of a spiritual butterfly, where we can flit from
succulent flower to flower, drinking of the nectar of
prayer. As we move on to feed from another, so too
we are running away from something that we find

blunted, deadened and cannot handle. There comes a time when we have to stop and find the holy place wherever we are, and we may be surprised to find that we have been carrying it with us all the time.

Meanwhile on our journey how do we derive sustenance from these holy places and open the doors for others to follow and search? As we gather the clutter of life around us we need to find that space where we can pray both physically and metaphorically. For myself I love the simplicity of Romanesque and Norman architecture – the glories of Tournos in France and Norwich Cathedral in England, the Abbey of Bec in Normandy, and the simplicity of the church there which was once the stable, uncluttered by the trappings of the centuries. I need the silence and stillness which that brings, and a place where generations have offered prayer. It is not a nostalgia but a living reality, not to escape from this world but a facing up to the real one dimly reflected in the silent architectural glories around us. Just as we need these holy places to pray, so too do we need the simple skills of seeing through them as aids to prayer, pointers along the way, to rest in but not to stay for ever, where we can ask questions of stone and seek to understand why and to uncover the glories therein.

So no matter where you find your holy place, do not expect to rest there in this life. Be prepared to move on and make way for others. The place we are all looking for will not in all probability be found in this world, but the real joy is that you are seeking.

4

People

One Sunday morning, when I was staying with a vicarage family in Suffolk, I awoke to the sound of bird song and footsteps on the gravel. I looked out of the window just as the footsteps stopped. It was the Vicar coming back from the church after the early morning service. He had stopped some distance from the house and was having a conversation, a conversation with the vicarage cat, which had paused in its morning ablutions and was apparently listening, with head cocked to one side, to every word that Ian was saying. Here was a man who not only had time for God and people but for animals as well. It is surprising the channels we find open us to God, and through people we can find ways to an understanding of God, often in quite surprising and unlikely people.

The great saints of every age serve as beacons of prayer and the devotional life, and many aspire to their example. For most of us perhaps this is pitching things too high, often leading to damaging disappointment in our failure. Too often with well known people, famous saints or footballers, they remain distant and out of our experience, only made known through legend and television. If we were to meet them face to face we might well be surprised, just as we might well have been surprised when they decided to televise the House of Commons. Even through television, no matter how revealing the personality may be, there is still a veil and we cannot meet the real person. So we begin to make our own images and assumptions about this or that aspect of their personalities, and put onto them things we really wish they would be like, beginning to believe that is the way they are, when it is in fact all a figment or wish from our own imagination. Imagine what the years that separate us from the saints of old have done for their reputation!

God works through people to bring us to prayer. While still looking at the example of the Saints, and looking at their writings and experience we need also to follow the example of those set around us today. I do not mean the Michael Ramseys, Mother Teresas or Pope John Pauls, but the people in our own communities of faith, which is one reason alone for being the member of a worshipping community. The influence of these people may have been working on us through the years, though we have failed to recognize it. The interesting thing is that they come in all shapes and sizes and all types, and there is no blueprint. They need not necessarily be people whom we actually like!

Perhaps I was too young to judge, but the Headmistress at my junior school did not seem to take the Assemblies from the set school service book – rather battered, and on poor quality paper – in a manner which really conveyed any feeling of belief in what she was saying. It was a little like our early education, when we learnt everything parrot fashion, and it ended with a uniform and definite "AMEN".

We did not even know what the word meant. Attempts to deepen the spiritual input at the school were introduced on Wednesday mornings, when the local rector would come in and stand in front of the only warm stove in the building. He would talk to us about the things of Jesus and then we would sing, unaccompanied, "All Things Bright and Beautiful" while he swayed backwards and forwards, making these accessions for the only bout of seasickness which I have suffered on dry land. The poor man was not comfortable in this situation, and it was not helped by the fact the Headmistress spent her time checking and "Tut, tutting" over the registers. He was remote and he was the man of God.

At secondary school the spiritual life was not really enhanced by a Welsh Rugby-playing R.E. teacher who insisted upon filling us with facts from the Old Testament. "One eye's higher than the other", to remind us of the Prophet Isaiah; and "A mosquito" to help us recall the shepherd from Tekoa who rejoiced in the name Amos! The lady with the "bun" hairstyle and steel spectacles, clad in warm tweeds, had a go on religion with the less able classes, as if they were more in need of the experience than the rest of us. If you were not in the "a" or "b" stream you received more religious education than others! Religion stopped at school formally in the second or third year, and was only introduced momentarily in the words of the hymns at the morning Assemblies and with the loud and united "Amen". We still did not know what it meant, and did not have the confidence to ask. You did not question, you were taught not to question. The experience of a lower-middle-class secondary education in the late 'fifties and early 'sixties did nothing to help one approach prayer with any understanding. It was never spoken about, although we were expected to do it in uniform lines, standing in an assembly hall while the occasional fidgetter got a backhander from the nearest master, who was trying to keep order in the ranks.

From an unlikely source came the angel of salvation, Mary the Policeman's daughter dragged my brother and me along to the confirmation classes, with the help of a bribe of fish and chips afterwards! The Rector in the village had changed, and there was now a quiet man who had worked hard in London. He was single and wore a black cloak and black beret. I remember little about the confirmation classes, and even less about the confirmation, but I do remember this man who spoke with some authority about praying, and I have prayed morning and night whatever and wherever since his lessons. It became apparent too that attendance at church was necessary for the spiritual life, and so we were enlisted, I with more success than my brother, into the village choir. On winter days we sat in the chancel, keeping warm by expensive oil-filled electrically heated pipes, and firmly saying "Amen" at the relevant moment... still not knowing what it meant.

Here there were people who prayed and had been praying for many years. Nellie, Jim and Jack had all sung in the choir, with lessening musical and more damaging effect as the years went by, but still they set an example of discipline in prayer, and were faithful in "public and private worship". They never stopped to discuss why or what prayer was, but they were living examples of those who believed and prayed. They were never destined to be singled out as great spiritual leaders, they were unspectacular and shy, humble people, and they prayed and set an example to all who came to see, or who saw them walking, with increasing difficulty as the years went by, to church each Sunday. Their presence registered to the world that they were at prayer by the tolling of the church bell each service.

It lacks humility in saying it, but my contact with the clergy has not always been an immediate inspiration to the prayerful life. A very earnest and godly man he may have been, but another of the early vicars I had contact with was someone who never seemed to be able to communicate in words that hit the mark. He had trained at Ridley Hall in Cambridge, then considered to be an evangelical college. The poor chap never mastered communication with his fellow man, so how he communicated with the Almighty must have been a something between them both. You must expect to isolate yourself from a community if you catch the milkman on the doorstep and have him kneeling in prayer for half an hour, and you cannot expect Joe, who has been ploughing the fields for years, to stop while the Vicar kneels down by the side of the tractor to pray for thirty minutes. In church at services the prayers could outdo the sermon, and wander from Persia to Peterborough, stopping at every problem in between before ending. Odd, eccentric, ardent, sincere he may have been, but he never seemed to give people confidence in their faith and courage in their prayer. If it all took that long for him, what chance did we have?

Once again light was shed from an unexpected source. Bob had been coming to this church for many years. Now Bob was a small man with a large family. His wife came to church occasionally, but Bob was always there. On a Friday and Saturday evening he would be at the village club really enjoying himself to the full, and telling a tale along with the rest. At work he could outswear anyone who upset him. On Sunday he was in church on his knees and saying his prayers. If anyone in the village was in need, Bob was the first there. I am not saying his example was any worse or any better than the ardent Vicar, but Bob was a member of the village, a local, and for all his faults he maintained his faith, often despite the Vicars he came across. On the odd occasion we could persuade him to do the intercessions, usually because we wanted to get to the cricket match after the 3.00 p.m. evensong or home to lunch at a reasonable hour. We heard prayers that though short were profound and came from the heart. Bob was one of four people who influenced me in that community. Mrs. R., also a Churchwarden, was faithful and true to the end, and she cared for two elderly sisters, who lived opposite us in a little cottage without any facilities but they prayed. One was blind and the other did all the work, but together they prayed, and it was a privilege to share in their moments of prayer.

Years later the chastening experience of theological college gave me an insight into the many traditions that came under the heading of prayer, and the many and varied types of people, including myself, who were to try to help others pray?... And I still did not know what AMEN meant!

There was an accepted discipline at college, it was in the spirit of the thing rather than the law! The accepted pattern was morning and evening prayer in the college chapel, and the Eucharist whenever possible. There are those who go to great lengths still for a daily "mass". The spiritual leader of this community, the college principal, was always there, and indeed it was a discipline that I did not find difficult to accept, and to a great extent enjoyed. Much to my surprise this was not the feeling of the majority of the students who steadfastly stayed away, presumably following their own prayer life in whatever way they thought possible. There were times when we had college debates about the matter, and the attendance was greatly enhanced at the time of exams, but there was never what I recall as being a full turn out! The college principal was a near Old Testament figure, and like so many clergymen I have met had a communication problem with ordinary mortals, but there was no doubt that Reggie said his prayers and was desperate to encourage others to do the same. The problem was that at college not all were of the same religious churchmanship as he was, let alone the same cultural background, and the mixing of evangelicals and high churchmen was not an easy alliance. It was one that was nurtured purely for financial reasons rather than the traditions of the college itself.

It was, however, Reggie who drew me to Sarum,

and there was something about him that I found helped me in my prayer life. I do not remember much about what he said, but to me there was an integrity in his public prayers. It was he who showed me the way to address God openly and without wrapping things up in theological language, and in many ways set me free to talk with God.

Theological College and my fellow students taught me a great deal of humility for the differing feelings people had about prayer. There was no doubt in my mind, by the time I left, that it had to be done and that time had to be found for it.

I have been saddened by meeting with some church leaders who hide behind their office and fail to have the confidence to reveal their true selves. This has often seemed the case with many bishops and other church leaders that I have come across. It may be, of course, that they are revealing their true selves, but I have often felt that I have been confronted with someone playing at the office rather than being the person in that office. There have of course been some notable exceptions, and these have not worn the mantle of their office, or the fact that they pray a great deal, on their sleeves.

We do go back to the age-old problem of investing in other people how we feel they ought to be, rather than seeing them as they really are and as perhaps God would have them be. If only we could see ourselves as other people see us! In the end, no matter how inspired or guided by other people, we have to sort out a prayer life of our own, while also trying to use it with the channel of prayer within a church.

The man who offered me my first curacy had been a Spitfire pilot in the war, and had a large and gregarious family. He loved his family, his job and the family dog, along with all the people in his care. The tradition in which he had been brought up as a clergyman, and his military training, failed to release him from the set prayers and those written in books by others, but he did have a knack of choosing prayers written by others which spoke to the present generation and released him. We prayed as Vicar and Curate every morning and night, along with the verger, who came in very firmly at the appropriate moment with the "AMEN". I don't believe Paul ever found time during the day for special times of prayer, and I know he found intimate groups difficult, but he said his prayers and was strengthened by them, as well as strengthening others.

One day we were sitting in the Lady Chapel just beginning to say evensong, when a bustling group of short and dumpy Welsh ladies came scuttling in and, quickly finding the prayer book page, joined heartily in the normally quiet evensong. They were immediately at home with the service and scurried out after the final blessing, having joined in heartily and with meaning to every AMEN, while Paul and I sat for our normal fifteen minutes' silence. It was as if we had been visited by a flight of Angels; and perhaps that was what they were. Their presence had brought a great deal to our prayers that night.

Within parishes there are many people who pray at home and seldom speak about it. All too often these are depicted in literature and films as quiet, willowing people who are rather "sweet". If you do not fit into that category it does not matter, for you do not have to be like that to say your prayers at home. Trapped by the discipline of their backgrounds, many hang on to the prayers as set for the church and state in the prayer book, and find release for their own prayers within these.

It has not been saints or gurus who have convinced me to go on when I was ordained and going through a difficult patch in my prayer life, but those who came to church regularly and whom I knew well. They were not often quiet people or what you would call "holy", just very ordinary, but had discovered their need of God. Sometimes in their daily life these were difficult characters to handle, and they held fearsomely responsible positions, but still they came and prayed.

Deservedly I have been brought up with a start in the strange world of radio and television in which I move from time to time. For some reason in the early days I felt that no one with whom I was working was at all sympathetic with any of the religious views that I held, but when I began to get to know them better I was amazed at the number of people in the industry who went to church and said their prayers. Serves me right for my arrogant thoughts! Some too suffer from the classical ideals of what men and women of God should be, and feel inferior because they could not be like one of the saints of every age. Indeed, I remember having a discussion with David Attenborough, who felt that the men of God should be mystical and quiet and not like my noisy self. It is good to be made to think, but then we have to find self and learn to live with it.

The Professional People of Prayer, the clergy, must suffer from feelings of isolation, and that they are the only ones saying any prayers, and we know of course this is not true. A continual recitation of the formularies and prayers of the books can trap you into a prayer life which is rigid and not free to grow. The gift of prayer is not limited to the professional in any way. It is freely given to all, and is possible for all, although in many differing ways. The people who inspire us and lead us there need not be the famous, but those around us who also share some sympathy in communicating with God.

5

Showing Others The Way

We often lose sight of man made in the image of God, and God the Creator. Perhaps we forget that as parts of God's creation then each individual is also part of Him, so that we should not be surprised when the most unlikely people, as seen through our eyes, come up with surprising questions and insights into prayer.

Never having been famed for being a quiet clergyman, I was somewhat surprised to be asked to take the Confirmation Retreat for sixth formers from a leading Public School. I worked diligently at preparing my material, mainly autobiographical, and spent some time wondering what to wear. On these occasions, especially in meeting young people, there is a balance between what you would normally wear – in my case jeans and a dog collar – and what they would want you to wear – in this case a cassock and dog collar – otherwise you might be accused of being trendy!

But how do we actually set about the task? In this chapter we will go into some detail as to how I try to help others find a footing on the ladder of prayer.

I delivered the addresses in the morning, and divided the afternoon up into time for the young men to come and see me at ten-minute intervals. I took a good book and settled down for a peaceful afternoon's reading. At precisely the time appointed there was a knock on the door, and so it went on at ten-minute intervals throughout the afternoon, by which time I was exhausted. They were certainly interested in many aspects of God, but especially in praying. The problem was to help them see that they had comprehended so much already, and really needed not to look too deeply but to have some awareness of the power of prayer. Passing knowledge about prayer is in part helping them realize that they are all on the journey anyway.

The Disciples asked Jesus to "Teach us how to pray", and we learn for the first time of the Lord's Prayer, one I often use when all else seems to escape me. "No one talks about prayer these days", is often a cry I hear from churches and church groups as I go around the country. This I find hard to believe entirely, although there can be a natural reluctance to set down fast rules and regulations about prayer which will suit everyone. We only have to look at the multiplicity of expressions of faith within the Church to see that the way some people pray would not necessarily suit everyone; indeed, some may feel alienated by some styles and methods of prayer. We each have to find a "way", that being common in part to all also allows us an expression of our faith that will support and sustain us. There are many ways, and indeed as I write I have said the quiet prayer asking God to guide what I say and to offer some inspiration, an immediate or, as some call it, an arrow prayer, the sort of prayer you might offer while cooking supper or washing up!

For some the tradition of prayer has been a part of

the rhythm of family life. Indeed, many learn about prayer from their families along with other facts of life. For others the way is well supported, and often in both cases the path is not sustained by the regular attendance at a church. There can be little doubt that if we see something is important to our parents then, although we may not always agree with them, we respect their feelings, and sometimes in later life come to concur with what they were trying to express. They set the standard by which we may live or choose to live, although we may not follow it all the time. There is that natural period of rebellion as we seek to break the umbilical cord and lead our own lives, when many of us reject the ways of our parents, but hopefully we will still respect the things that they hold dear. Prayer may not be important to them, and many people come to prayer by different roots.

As parents with children many church-going mums and dads try to help their young children with prayers at night, and although it may perhaps be lessening, there can be little doubt that helping young children to say a few prayers by the bedside can help them in later life. The danger is that we might disillusion them if they discover that it is not real for us, but only something that children do. The ideals we try to pass on to children have to be backed up by action, and so showing the way at the bedside must be followed up by the expression of our faith in some form of attendance at worship in a Christian community. Likewise, reading and study of the Bible in the home can lead to a deeper understanding of prayer, and will be seen as a beacon to the young that this is something we take seriously and which needs to be nurtured. The inclusion of children at adult services helps them to see that Mother and Father take the matter seriously, and although in the early days the children may not understand what is going on, time and regularity, along with familiarity and support, can lead them to a deeper understanding.

All too often there is a call to take children away from the main service and usher them into a side room or hall for Sunday School. To be honest, I am not sure of the value of this for everyone. My own experience was bereft of any membership of a Sunday School, as it was of any parental instruction. The vexed question of children in church seems to upset many people one way or the other, and a good Anglican compromise is often sought. The children come in for the first part of the service and are then ushered out for the sermon, to return in time for a blessing as the parents come to the altar rail to receive the Sacrament. The only problem about all this is the matter of timing. We never really know how long the sermon or the hymns will be, the poor Sunday School teachers may not be ready when we are ready, and vice versa. Will the person who is supposed to go and collect the children remember? The weather intervenes and there is a downpour, so do we let them cram into the porch giggling and generally becoming more miserable by the moment, or do we let them in to rush to their parents at the moment of consecration thus disturbing everyone's peace? There are an enormous number of combinations that work for some and not others. A lot depends on the actual buildings, the availability of staff, the numbers of children, the nature of the congregation, but perhaps most of all the ability of the leader of the main service to cope! Not every leader of a service is a natural performer able to cope with the multitude of things which happen at the back of the church. The congregations in the main have their backs to whatever is happening, and those who lead the service see all the comings and goings which are often a necessary part of a service in church.

My own feelings are simple to express. If the parents wish to bring their offspring to the service, no matter what age, then they are welcome. If little Aaron decides that it is time for playing up, then all Mum or Dad has to do is pick him up and take him to the car or to the Vestry or to some other place where he can be pacified. If he can't be pacified then take him home and try again next week. It can't be impossible for people to exercise a little humanity and commonsense to help families worship together. There must be enough parental support within most congregations to see that the young Mum and Dad are helped as much as possible to cope with their children. Perhaps it is the natural English reserve not to get involved which holds many people back from offering a helping hand. It does not take much to realize that Paul is in the Vestry with Aaron again, and that he may like to receive communion, which he could do if I go and look after Aaron while he receives. A lot of the so-called problems of children in church can be solved by a little common humanity and sense, and indeed a lot of congregations do cope very well.

Many people express the feeling that regularity in

a baby's life is all-important and that there needs to be a sort of rhythm. This then is why we need to help the child realize that part of that rhythm is paying attention to God in prayer, and this can be helped by regular attendance in church. Likewise, those who organize services need to realize that familiarity in services also helps congregations of all ages. I am not convinced that a pattern that alters every Sunday actually helps people with their prayer and worship, no matter how exciting the menu may be.

It must be obvious to the reader that I have no children of my own, and in some respects perhaps I am seeking an ideal world, where the family can worship together without let or hindrance, and where everything is done "decently and in order" as St Paul suggests. What I am trying to express is a concern that we need to pray together as a community for all ages, and so the sooner we start our young off on that journey, with confidence that it is a group activity as well as an individual one, the better.

Sunday Schools may help, but perhaps they need to be at a time other than that of the main service. All too often they can become a dumping ground for children on a Sunday morning while Mum and Dad settle to various jobs at home, picking them up in time for Sunday lunch, "an escape route from anarchy", as one parent explained to me. Sunday Schools open the door for some, but if their parents do not hold them by the hand as they walk through it, the children may trip over the mat, get up and run away home. Then there is the danger of the thought of prayer resting simply at the Sunday School stage and never maturing with age and experience. All too often after Sunday School there is very little support for those enquiring further and needing support, and so the ideas never mature, and although we grow up our image and perception of the relevance of prayer stays in the Sunday School image.

In my own experience there was no parental initiative to instigate the idea of praying. To tell the truth, I cannot remember when the idea was first introduced, if it was not at the village school which I attended. The 1944 Education Act was followed by the letter by the Headmistress, a sharp Welsh lady, with morning Assembly which consisted of a hymn, unaccompanied, and the same prayers morning after morning, from the specially prepared schools service book. Later in life I realized that it was a sort of mini matins. There was no Bible reading as far as I can remember. The local Vicar came in every Wednesday morning to tell us something about Jesus, and from the combination of the two events we were supposed to "get" religion and thrive. On Ascension Day we crossed the Village High Street to go to the local church for a special service, and that was that; but at least it was something!

A change of Rector and the arrival of a new Village Policeman gave rise to some Confirmation Classes to which, as I have said earlier, we were encouraged to go with the offer of fish and chips afterwards by the said policeman's daughter. If I gained nothing else from these classes, then the fact that I should pray each day was a jewel that I will always treasure. I started praying at the age of eleven and have not stopped. The manner and the style have often varied, but there have been nightly prayers ever since. They may not be sophisticated and they may not be articulate, but they have been offered to God.

So how do we respond when someone asks us to teach them how to pray? I sometimes wonder if there is some significance in the age of the disciples, and indeed of Jesus Himself, when the first disciples demanded the answer of Him. My Father says that no one gets any commonsense until they are twenty-five, so give or take a few years perhaps this is when some people begin to think more seriously about life, a time perhaps filled with the arrival of the responsibilities that age brings. Reflecting upon the times this challenge has been thrown down to me in my own ministry, a confusing array of answers springs to mind. On a visit to my Theological College I once asked the same question of Michael Ramsey, or at least I asked him to tell us something about prayer. I remember my question, it was very simple, ''What about Prayer?'' The eyes closed, the bushy eyebrows seemed to curl, and there was a long meditative silence!

As I have related to you earlier, my awareness of some force in the world other than what we could comprehend came before my awareness of Jesus, and later in life I came to understand that this force is God. Jesus, on whom so much of our prayers are focused, came later. Anyone who asks about prayer may well have some seed of faith, some spark which they wish to nurture and build upon. The person who has turned to you and asked the question may well see you as a person who knows something about prayer. You have something, some insight of which they want a part. The responsibility is enormous: to encourage the quest but not to guarantee the result.

I always offer the caution not to expect too much, no blinding flash or instant solutions to life's questions. It may seem obvious enough, but it does need to be said. How often have you heard the cry, "I've tried praying about it, but that does not seem to help"? There are after all many kinds of prayer.

Perhaps the most common to us all is the **petition**, the asking prayers. A request to God or Jesus, or to one of the saints to bring to the attention of God a certain need which requires fulfilling. "Dear God, my father is ill, please make him well", "My finances are in a state, please help me sought them out", "Please bring Peace", and so on, all of them relevant and all of them just prayers. Sometimes for a person to turn to prayer means they are at their wits' end and there is nothing else to try. It is a pity to wait until then. In my own experience, in the early days my prayers of petition were often for other people, and I had a slightly selfish feeling when addressing God in this way to help me personally. If God knows all, then He knows what I want, so is there any need to ask?

The Petition prayer almost demands an answer of God, and I remember many debates over the years based on the theme, "Does God answer prayer?" You could write a book or two on the debates that question has caused in groups throughout Christendom. The awful truth is that so often we want God to give the answer we wish for, and when we do not receive it then disillusionment can set in.

Reasoning things through, though, can often restore our faith somewhat.

There are those who can claim that God has miraculously answered their prayers in some dramatic way, and they joyfully shout the news from the rooftops – and who wouldn't if there had been a dramatic turn-around in someone's illness which has meant a reprieve from death or some such seeming tragedy. We all love success and want to share in it. This is human nature, but beware – not everyone receives the answer they desire, and the joyful crowing may exile someone who feels God is not on their side. Does God need that sort of shouting from the rooftops when these events take place, especially when they can turn into stumbling blocks for others? Then there is the nature of the answer that God has given. If we feel it is the right one, was it wrought by some dramatic effect, or was it forged in silence? Perhaps in the event itself there is a key to how we should accept the answer that God has given in response to our petition.

Many people make petitions to God on a regular basis for the same reason. It can become an obsession and perhaps block out the channel by which God has already given an answer. In personal matters especially it may be wise to share your petition to God with another, or perhaps a Prayer Group anonymously or, if your group is a close one, then openly. Asking others to share your prayer of petition can help with the burden you may be carrying. This takes sensitivity, for some may see the answer to the petition as being present while the person who offers the original petition may well be blind to it, and to rush in with the answer as you see it may not help them. It is important that the realization of the answer must be perceived by the person who makes the original petition.

For many people who struggle with prayer, membership of a group or confidence to join a group is a long way off, and they will struggle for some time in the wilderness before they feel strong enough to move into such a meeting. Attendance at church can help bridge the gap, and for many is sufficient, as so often the prayers that are used include thoughts, words and feelings that individuals have themselves, and so they feel a part of a praying community. There still needs to be space and courage for the individual to pray.

Each Sunday churches offer prayers of petition to God on a grand scale for Peace, Relief of Famine etc., etc. It is as if we are calling for God to intervene in a grossly dramatic way and suddenly put things to rights, without humanity itself lifting a finger to do anything. This is a banal way of interpreting the worthy prayers of millions of Christian folk and is the wrong interpretation. Prayer does perhaps do two things: it can focus our attention on the needs of the world and it expresses our concern to God to do something about the problems. So often, on less than deep analysis, we can see that the answers lie within the communities of nations and the individual will. Such prayers strengthen the individual resolve to be a part of a greater whole looking for the welfare of humanity and indeed of the world. They help keep things in perspective, and help us to realize that we are not isolated in our desires. By sharing a common petition, they give strength to the individual will. However, we still look for a response from God, which is natural, and we do see that response when the human will is touched to respond to needs in many ways, either in the life of an individual like Mother Teressa, or in the generosity of nations in responding to the many appeals that arise from time to time. We surely have more ability than we are prepared to use to solve some of these great problems that persist in the world, but on the other hand there are those which seem to have little or no answer that we can find, and which may well be with us for generations as the result of natural disasters.

Returning to the personal petition, the ones which more often than not bring people to prayer, ''Anything you ask in my name and it will be given you'' challenges when we do not seem to get the response that we wish. In all these prayers of petition we need to add the rider, ''Your will be done'', for so often what we want may not be the way that God wants for us. Our petitions need to be nailed to the Cross, and, although often repeated, left to work out as God would have them do.

For those who turn to God in prayers of petition need to be bold enough to ask for the world and courageous enough to accept that the answer may not be always as we would wish. Offer the prayer of petition to God and then let it go. ''Your will be done.''

In some respects we really have things the wrong way round. I have heard it said that **thanksgiving** is the beginning of prayer. As I sit in the study and write, occasionally looking out of the window at the trees and the swallows, hearing the bird song and seeing my neighbour's cats playing in the garden as the sun shines out of a blue sky, then I feel there is a great deal to be thankful for. On another day, when the bills have arrived and the bank statement looks none too healthy, and there is not much work in the pipeline, with the rain coming down hard and the car on its last legs, I feel less than thankful and ill at ease and less than confident. So it is for most of us a strange mixture of good and bad things that we have to balance in life. My simple faith in a loving God tells me that all these things are transient, and that I must work towards perfection and a place in that mysterious heaven; yet in the meantime I have to work my way through the maelstrom of life. It is so easy to forget to say **Thank You**. I do my best to write notes to people who have been kind to me in one way or another, or have entertained me at some function. At Christmas time I always remind the children to write and thank relatives and friends for their gifts. A THANK YOU completes the gift.

It goes without saying that it can be no negative thing to start by thanking God for all the gifts that we have, even if personally we may not feel there is much to be thankful for. There must be very few people who cannot find anything to be thankful for at some point in their lives, even if they have to look hard. We have the gift of life, a new day, friends and family. Others may not be so fortunate, but if we can find one thing to thank God for each day then prayer can take on an extra strength. Sunday worship takes on some of this thankfulness in the hymns and prayers that are offered, but on a more intimate personal level it is no bad thing each day to find some small thing to thank God for. It starts us off on a positive note upon which we can build. As always it is best to keep things within the realms of our own experience and not try to cast the net too wide. Look at personal things or the things of nature to help point the way to a feeling of thankfulness; then we may come to an understanding that God does indeed have an awareness of what we need before we ask.

In praying perhaps we sometimes take on too much and expect too much. We seem to want to cling to matters of prayer rather than leaving them for a while and letting time take the burden. What we all desperately seek is answers, and it cannot be said often enough that all too often the answer is already with us. It is folly, though, not to ask. The manner in which we ask need not be wrapped up in fancy or theological words. The simple truth, pondered upon, is often enough.

I have purposely steered clear of any attempt at pointing the way to prayer using other people's words of the words of the saints, or prayer books and the "Hymns Ancient and Modern". There is no doubt that all these have a contribution to make, putting into utterable words the thoughts and feelings that we have.

God understands our own unintelligible utterances, I am sure. There is no correct language with which to address prayers to God, no one language has the monopoly. It does help in public praying to be able to make sense of what is being prayed about in the weekly intercessions, and a lack of preparation which takes us from Paddington to

Poland in one sentence is more likely to confuse than to inspire. Careful preparation and thoughtfulness usually help the congregation tune into the leader's thoughts.

We have glimpsed at **Thankfulness** and **Petition** as forms of prayer. As a practical step it can also help to **keep a journal** of those things for which we are asking God's help, and those things for which we are thankful. When praying for people, simply keeping a list of names and running over them from time to time helps not only to retain them in our thoughts and prayers, but also reminds us of friendships and acquaintances that can so easily be lost. A parish priest has no end of people to remember, and I still keep the lists of names, no details, of people with whom I have come into contact over the years. It is surprising how fresh the relationship seems when you meet them again after a long gap. To carry this further, making notes about the topic of your intercession is no bad thing and can often help in assessing your own development into the prayer life.

As this life develops there are other ways which can deepen the sense of prayer that comes with practice. Some parishes have prayer groups, others try retreats on prayer, when a small group of people go away to a retreat house with a leader, often imported for the occasion, to think about prayer. New and deeper ways of praying are often discovered, meditation being one of the most fundamental. It is something that many people do not find themselves immediately at ease with, and it certainly needs some concentration and practice. Surroundings and atmosphere can be important, but

I guess few would wish to follow St Simon of the Stylities, who spent much of his life meditating at the top of a pole. This may be well for the extreme aesthetic, but most of us have to keep our feet firmly on the ground to feel at home at all. Many religions have an expression of meditation, and indeed as far as our human brain is concerned it is probably a very good way of helping our overworked minds relax a little when we are not asleep. At College our Principal exercised some meditation after evensong each day. We would sit in the chapel, very comfortably on our chairs, with our feet a little apart, and with our hands resting on our knees, and simply close our eyes and sit very quietly, not thinking of anything in particular. It is surprising how difficult it is to disengage the brain from the multiplicity of things which have come across our paths in the course of a day. Perhaps the end of the day was not the best time to try.

For some the addition of music helped their meditation, or some object upon which to ponder or discover. The Eastern Church uses Icons, but for some it will the relic of some holy saint of perhaps a Crucifix, Cross, Chalice or some other religious object. Our group at College once used a chalice, and we set it in the middle of our circle, gently focusing upon it for some time. One member fell asleep, another left through boredom, but others stood the couse. I am not sure that any of us achieved a meditative state, but it did have a relaxing effect on some of us.

Another aid of course are the works of the mystics, and there is no doubt that the writings of such people as Mother Julian of Norwich have helped many people come to a greater understanding of prayer through meditation. There are those who have been gifted in being able to put into words their thoughts and feelings on their meditations. For others a walk in the hills or a quiet place in the countryside can open the door to meditation, and even in the factory and office some are able to find places to ponder, if they cannot do so at home.

One of the problems is undoubtedly that not everyone around you will appreciate your feelings and leave you enough space and peace. Even escapes into the country will find locked churches, so that you cannot go in and simply sit there, quietly to offer a few prayers or just ponder. These are deeper matters than I wish to go into in this chapter.

The matter of praying is a very practical fact of any Christian life. There is a great danger that you compare yourself with so and so, or some saintly figure, or even the Vicar, and feel that you are not on the same level as they are. They seem to have the key to it all. This is not the case. The channel of prayer is for us all to use if we feel called to try. I would hope that we do not leave the effort of prayer to some crisis in life, but begin a practical look at ways of praying with **Thankfulness** and **Petition**. The prayers of childhood, if we are lucky enough to have had a glimpse of them, may well be a way in, but failing that and having a person whom you feel you can approach for advice, how about simply asking God, "Father teach me to pray"?

I simply believe that no one is excluded from calling on God in prayer. The very fact that the idea of prayer may have crossed your mind lends rise to the possibility of the seeds of Faith. Understanding, as far as any of us achieve that, may come much later. It is an exercise for the old and the young, and no one need feel excluded from the right to pray unless they exclude themselves. In our school we had a picture of the famous Holman Hunt figure of Christ with a lamp in his hand knocking at the door, and that is all we have to do. It is good if there are a few people around to help us.

For those who have practised the discipline of prayer for many years there is the challenge of finding freshness and vigour time and time again. Reading and worship help fuel the fire, and indeed so does membership of a prayer group. We need ever be sensitive of the needs of new members, and not to make groups exclusive clubs of like-minded people. Neither should we lose in a mass of arguments the principles by which each groups stands. There may be need within one congregation for several groups of different flavours to which people can attach themselves and feel at home. The approaches are numerous, and a church should never feel that the poor Vicar can service them all; but he can benefit from your prayers for him.

Praying is quite the least spectacular aspect of our Christian ministry which we all have. Some say their prayer is their work, and carrying that idea into the daily routine is no bad thing: offering our whole lives to God. For others a piece of sculpture, a building, a work of art, is a form of living prayer that inspires our faith. These are refined limits. Most people want simply to know how to pray. I can only advise you to start from where you are. Ask God to help you, spend time thinking about what you wish to pray about. Make notes of topics for your prayers. They can be divided into many categories. Don't crowd your thoughts, and keep things simple. Find a space in the day and a quiet corner, and begin with the Lord's Prayer. There we are: you have started!

6

Silence

There cannot be many places where we can meet with complete silence, a deep and still silence that rests the mind. Prayer benefits from the use of silence, and I once tried to find this with a desire to become a Benedictine Monk. I found a wall of silence.

There is a picture that we all have of the peaceful tranquillity and road to silence that we can find in some church buildings, at least those not plagued with the noisy tourist! We come across it, appreciate it for the moment, and then move on. It is really quite difficult to find silence and then live with it for a while. I remember at Theological College we set about raising money for some cause or another outside College life, and many activities we called upon to help raise the necessary funds. Our group came upon the idea of a "Hush In", that was a sponsored silence, and we were able to encourage a lot of young people to come and take part. For most of them it was a different experience from anything they had ever encountered before.

It is very difficult though to find a spot where you can be completely silent. The Hush In was held in a town hall on a Saturday, and we had the constant noise of traffic going by outside. Most churches in towns have busy roads near them, and even in the countryside there is the noise of aircraft and agriculture, so that you cannot find the silence. Sometimes in the dead of night I do wake up and find that all is silent, really silent and peaceful – and then the fridge switches itself on in the kitchen, so you can't really win. In the city this quest for silence is very difficult to achieve.

What is it about the idea of silence which attracts some and frightens off others? Is it the fear of being alone or of having time to think?

At one level I really believe that silence is a good therapy for the mind, not at any religious level but purely at a practical one. Just think about it. There we are: your mind is working immediately, every moment that we live we see things, smell things, taste things, touch things and hear things, and all these activities are processed by the mind. Probably the most sensitive and used activity is hearing. It is one of the first we achieve as a baby, and the last to go when we die. All the time sounds are being fed into the mind via our ears, and the brain interprets these sounds to which we can if we wish respond. We can refrain from touching, we can decide not to taste or smell, and if we close our eyes we can refuse to see, but it is very difficult to stop hearing and not to listen, although we can control our response to what we hear. So if we impose an environment upon ourselves which is silent, then this part of the brain or mind perhaps has a chance to rest.

My primary school Headmistress had a saying, ''Empty Vessels make the most Noise''. I wonder if she was partly right! However, we live in times when, if we tend to find a silent spot, we immediately begin to think of ways of filling it. The radio or television goes on as soon as we arrive home. Even the journey to work can now be filled with sound with the advent of the Walkman. It is true that music soothes the troubled breast, but I feel that some of the "music" is less soothing than others, whether classical or pop. Even shops are filled with Muzak, either to speed the shopper on or, with subtle messages fed into the stream of sound, suggesting the day's best buys. Long-distance buses now have televisions on them, and so even there we fill any chance of silence with sound.

Electronically produced sounds tend to be more intrusive than the natural sounds of nature. Perhaps over thousands of years we have come to accept bird song and the sound of the wind, and we can lose them when we feel we need a little silence. Manmade sounds seem more troublesome, at least they do to me. There are places, though, to which we can escape.

There are mercifully throughout the country retreat houses, often run by churches, that are sanctuaries of silence. There are still monasteries and priories where the rule of silence, in parts of the house or area at least, is observed. The silence can sometimes be a shared experience, or it can be a solitary one, depending on your choice.

For my own part, as a young person I had a great deal of time on my own and became used to silence. Perhaps I took this privilege for granted, but then I knew no better. We lived deep in the Suffolk countryside, my parents worked, and my brother was away with his friends a great deal, so I found myself on my own, an experience which lasted some fourteen years until we moved into a village. In many ways this has affected the way I am now, a fairly solitary person who enjoys limited gregariousness and enjoys company, but who is close to very few people

Out of the silence that I experienced came an understanding and awareness that there is something in life, some controlling force over which we ourselves have no control. At one level it is called nature and at another level God. There are the natural things which happen, usually in a stunning silence. The change of the seasons, the blossoming of the flowers in spring, and the ripening of the crops. Little or no noise is associated with these activities of nature. There is an unperceived effort but they all take place in silence.

Conception, the moment the sperm breaks into the egg and fertilizes it, happens in silence. Wars end when a Treaty, a silent piece of paper containing silent written words, is signed, and the peace descends. How much more powerful a thing then than noise and activity is silence. There is, however, a balance. As the bread is baking silently in my oven at the moment there has been a certain amount of activity and noise which has gone into the process. The corn seed was sown by a noisy machine, harvested by a noisy machine, ground by a noisy machine, and transported by noisy machines, before being kneaded with the yeast and water and left to rise in silence a couple of times, before baking in silence. The end result is born out of silence. The activity has helped produce the ingredients but the end result happens in silence. Silence has played a part.

This illusive silence, which we seem to find less and less of, has a part to play and we need to make room for it. This is part of the balance of life. St Benedict in his Rule, which some communities still follow, allows space for activity, noise and above all silence. Do we really need to have noise coupled with every activity? I am conscious that as I write on the word processor the machine is making a whirring noise, and my tapping at the keys makes a noise as well. I just wonder how many modern works of literature will achieve the greatness of a Shakespeare, who probably used a quill, rather more quiet than my machine.

I just want to make one more analogy as I struggle to express the productive quality of silence. For some years I worked as an Operating Theatre Technician in a local hospital. As anyone who has been a patient will tell you, hospitals are not that restful a place to be, there is always a little noise and activity, but amid the noise and activity the healing process actually takes place in silence. You do not hear the operation, you do not hear the process of healing nor the germs being destroyed – the good things are happening in silence. This silence, as are many other things, is in fact part of a balanced reality.

I would argue that our lack of the use of silence today, in a balanced whole of life, does little to enhance our human state or help us in our understanding of God. The use of silence in prayer can be a blessing, especially in public worship, when it is often under-used. Time and again I keep telling myself that not everyone is experienced or even talented enough, if those are the right words, to present prayers in public worship. Many seem to think that they have to fill every second with some petition, thanksgiving or other, instead of allowing a little measured silence. We become so bombarded with the presenter's thoughts, ideas and instructions to God that we often forget we have come to pray, and that prayer involves waiting as well as action.

In personal prayers there is more room for silence. Resist the temptation to fill the time that you may allow yourself for daily prayer with words or thoughts. Quite often it is a good idea to divide your week up into days when you pray about specific things, and then make a brief list of items you wish to pray about. Allow a pause or some silence between each prayer, or allow a few minutes' silence after the time you allow yourself to pray. Do not expect too much too soon. Just take a little step towards a great silence each time.

At a more organized level, the experience of a retreat can help a great deal. It is an idea that many people run away from, and indeed it is probably best that you do not decide to take part in one with a boisterous attitude. My experiences of retreats have not always been happy ones. So often the retreat house has been cold and the food abominable. So what does that matter, you may ask. Well it matters to me, and I find it very difficult to tackle anything new if I feel cold and badly fed. These things get in the way, and I am worrying about my tummy rather than working hard at the theme of the retreat. Many improvements have been made in retreat houses since the 'sixties when I first began to go on retreat. In desperation I have taken most of my more recent retreats in Abbeys in France, but I can name some very good places in Britain now.

Setting off on a journey to find a retreat where silence will play an important part, and believe me they do not always have that element of silence in them, may need the help of your local priest or someone he can recommend. Not all clergymen find retreats beneficial to their spirituality and you should not be surprised at that, it may not be part of yours. Some parishes organize their own retreats and invite a leader to come along to speak at certain times on a theme, allowing time for silence and prayer in between talks and services. The really experienced leader also allows time for healthy recreation in the afternoon, like a long walk or some other activity of your own choice which you can do alone. If you feel that perhaps a retreat with people you know well or reasonably well is not what you need, then you can join a retreat at any number of retreat houses which they themselves will organize and advertise in certain publications.

For many the mention of silence in any religious sense immediately conjures up monks and nuns parading in orderly fashion around their cloisters. In part this may be true, and indeed is the way it is, but it is not the whole. You can take an individual time out at an Abbey or Monastery and find some peace and quiet, joining in the daily round of worship and prayer which is at the centre of these institutions. I had a brief experience of the monastic life once, and was convinced that I wanted to become a monk.

There were various problems I was going through at the time, but I rationalized all that and still decided that this was what I wanted to do. Eventually arrangements were made and I took myself off to the Abbey. I'm not sure what really happened, but I was very unhappy. I came across a wall of silence, which was what I had been seeking, but instead of peace I found a restlessness that was disturbing, something was obviously wrong and this was not the way for me. I found that out very quickly, and returned to stay with some friends. That was an experience of silence which might well have been destructive if I had persevered in seeking it. Indeed silence, if you have too much of it, can lead to an isolation and all kinds of problems. It needs to be measured along with the rest of the things of life, but it should not be ignored.

Too much silence can suppress aggression and cause many personal problems. There needs to be an outlet for exercise, and some noise-making to help make the silences relevant. Keeping the balance is always the problem.

When I was a curate in Sherborne in Dorset, the Vicar and I always said evensong together at the end of the day unless it was one of our days off. After the service we would sit in silence for about fifteen minutes. The Lady Chapel was always cool, and there were one or two items to focus on if you were tired and needed a little diversion. These silences were used for reflection and sometimes pondering. They were never empty, but shared together they were made easier to cope with, and we both seemed to know automatically when we had had enough.

Perhaps some folk run away from silence because they find it too frightening, and yet silence does have a "sound" all of its own. I often think of the Simon and Garfunkel Farewell Concert I went to in Nice one summer. They sang their famous song, *The Sound of Silence*. After they had finished there was silence for a full minute before the audience erupted in applause. It was an amazing feeling, and a powerful silence which was building up the energy after appreciation of the song that had been sung. You know the saying about the "silence welling up inside you until it bursts". It was that sort of experience.

Then there is the silence which is called for just before the cameras or microphones are switched on in a broadcasting studio. Not only does it make sure that there is a smooth start for the programme, there is also a time in that silence which helps build up the energy so that you can release yourself into the item you have prepared.

I have set before you the scenario for an argument that out of silence a lot of good comes, a measured silence that is punctuated with other activities, but for which there is a part in your life. Silence used in the right way can be productive and good, and allow the mind time for rest, and the brain too. A time for replenishment and recharging, and indeed a time when the mind can be prepared to be receptive to new ideas and new concepts. Silence allows a little space in the brain, which stops all the activity keeping new thoughts and ideas out.

Have you ever spared time to think about the Resurrection? Not the arguments for or against the physical resurrection, but the fact that it happened in silence. Surely there was enough noise and suffering beforehand, but the actual event of the resurrection took place, as far as we know, in silence.

If we lose or give up the art of practising the use of silence, then we are in danger of being overwhelmed with a lot of noise and activity that silence can bring. It does not mean that we have to go about all our tasks in a pious state of silence, but we need to be aware of the gifts that the use of silence can give us, and to see that silence is part of our need and the natural rhythm of life, especially when it comes to prayer.

7

The Eucharist

The Eucharist or Holy Communion is an activity in which prayer, although often overlooked, forms a part of the whole.

How do we use prayer in the prayers of the Eucharist, and how can we prepare to place our own prayers in this context?

There is nothing so conservative as cult, is a saying which rings in my ears when we come to discuss any change within the church. In the 'seventies and 'eighties major changes have been seen in the styles of worship that have been adapted and adopted by many congregations at the behest of church leaders and theologians trying desperately to make worship relevant to succeeding generations. Perhaps the most sensitive of areas are covered by the revision of the Prayer Book, after many years of devoted use by the faithful. Whichever way we may feel about it, there is no doubt that to struggle with the change has been a good thing, for it has caused much debate and thinking amongst Christians and those interested in Faith.

We have ended up with the **Alternative Service Book, 1980,** "Services authorized for use in the Church of England in conjunction with The Book of Common Prayer" as the fly leaf informs us. For better, for worse, we have an alternative and it is widely used now in the Church of England. Other denominations too have struggled with change, not least the Methodist Church and the Roman Catholic Church, following the great Vatican Two council. For those outside the Church these changes may seem over-dramatized, but for many of the faithful much heart-searching and hurt was caused, as well as much stimulation.

For my own part I was caught up in the changes and found it easy to sympathize with the reformers, while not understanding much of the theological debate. I do remember one gathering at St Edmundsbury Cathedral when Canon Tony Jasper, a one-time leading light in the liturgical camp, enthused us to look at one of the series of drafts, waltzing up and down the aisle of the Cathedral in a white cassock. In lots of ways it made sense that we had change, because it did mean that we would be able to understand more about the services, especially the Eucharist, which probably proved the thorniest of all to deal with. This is my observation, it may not be a fact. Whatever happened, I was brought up on 1662 and easily transferred my allegiance to the new service, as I was not steeped in the traditions of the past. As I write for those who are searching and questioning, and because my knowledge of the ancient services is minimal, let us take a look at the **Eucharist** or **Holy Communion Rite A** as it is found at present in the Alternative Service Book. This is not to be a treatise on the pros and cons of the new service, but a look at the way I try to use each prayer as it is offered, and how I as a priest try to prepare for the service.

There are a couple of points that I wish to begin with. As the Priest, or, as the book suggests, the President, at the service I do literally see things from a different angle. Usually I am facing the congregation over a simple altar, and as I address the congregation in many parts of the service this is useful, because it causes me to move around less. Indeed, it is suggested in the notes of the service that the Eucharistic Prayer is a single prayer, and its unity may be obscured by changes of posture in the course of it.

The text demands that we do not flip from certain sections of the actual book to others at different parts of the service, i.e. for the Collect, Epistle and Gospel, and for the occasional preface, but I have found in practice that with careful marking these actions are no more or less than what we may have done with the Book of Common Prayer.

The most striking change, of course, is the language, and whereas we could read and listen to the Prayer Book almost as poetry, or at least as intrigued listeners to a language which was unfamiliar to us, the new services need much more ''presentation'. The Priest or President does need to be trained in the art of speaking in public, and using the text to help make the message of the prayers clear and their meaning understood.

I am going quite simply to take you with me through the service as I would use it at eight o'clock on a Sunday morning, without music, just using the text, and at each point commenting on how I try to use each prayer and how it helps point me in the direction of the service and my attention to God. This I hope will be useful for those who may be looking at the service as newcomers. It is not meant as a theological commentary, but more a way of my using the service and its parts as aids to prayer.

So let's get started. We need to turn to page 119 of the Alternative Service Book, The Order of Holy Communion Rite A. Before we even start the service we see that we have to look to another part of the book for An Appropriate Sentence. For this we may turn to the readings for the day, and in this instance, as I am writing about prayer, let us use the Collect and readings for Pentecost 14 and the Year 2 selection.

The Sentence may well set the theme for the rest of the service and then we are all greeted by the President, using a traditional greeting such as, "The Lord be with you" or the alternative "The Lord is here", to which we are encouraged to respond "and also with you" or "His Spirit is with us". It is as if both President and congregation are blessing each other, acknowledging and hoping for the presence of the Lord with both parties, opening the door of the service, breaking the ice if you like, and entering together upon a journey of faith. For the next thirty or forty minutes we are as one, paying attention to God, offering and receiving prayers and blessings.

We then pray together:

> Almighty God,
> to whom all hearts are open.

> all desires known,
> and from whom no secrets are hidden:
> cleanse the thoughts of our hearts
> by the inspiration of Your Holy Spirit,
> that we may perfectly love You,
> and worthily magnify Your holy name;
> through Christ our Lord. Amen.

In this prayer we face the truth about God, from whom we cannot hide, either physically or in our hearts and minds. To Him we are an open book, and there is no corner of ourselves He does not know, both the good and the bad. Our own personal struggles with the good and bad within us, God knows them all, and still he seeks us and calls us. Perhaps we can be tempted in this prayer to believe that we only look at the good things we desire, but we must remember that God sees our secret desires and they cannot be hidden, so we offer those things which we find troublesome to Him as well, openly and honestly, and ask His help on how to deal with them. Nothing is hidden from God, and even then He does not reject us, even if at times we are struggling with our rejection of Him.

We ask in this prayer for cleansing and for a helping hand in learning how most fittingly to love God and to show His glory by our lives. Here in this simple prayer we acknowledge our need of God, who knows everything about us, and we place our trust in Him to help us and strengthen us in the areas of our lives that we find difficult. We are not coming to the Communion as perfect people, but as imperfect people needing help and sustenance and forgiveness. We ask these things in the name of Jesus Christ.

This leads us nicely into the next section, the **Prayers of Penitence**. In fact the service book provides another place for these prayers after the intercessions. For my part I feel I am still approaching the Holy of Holies, and really do need to wipe my feet before I go any further, so for me this first stage is the best place to have the intercessions.

For some reason, and I have not discovered why, there is a chance to hear all or part of the Ten Commandments here. Perhaps on hearing them in full we can be reminded of our sins, those we have not repented of. We are reminded in the summary that the greatest sin is not putting God first, followed closely by the need to love of our neighbours.

The priest invites us to confess our sins, reminding us that Jesus Christ was sent to save us from our sins, and that in heaven He acts for us, working to bring us all to eternal life. So we move forward in penitence and faith, promising to try to improve ourselves.

The congregation is launched into the **Prayer of Confession**, so often with such gusto that it may seem it is a prayer of celebration rather than contrition! I like to leave a pause between the invitation to confess and the actual prayer of confession itself. In another chapter we will be looking at penitence in prayer, so let us stick to the practical side of things here. For my part I would like to hear the prayer said thoughtfully and rather quietly, as we reflect upon those things which we wish to leave at the foot of the Cross. We need to have made some preparation before coming to church, or at least as we have prepared for the service, to bring to this prayer any meaning for ourselves. For matters of conscience which have troubled us, or things we have done which are blatantly wrong, we do not make excuses nor do we try to analyze them in this prayer. There is no time. We simply face the facts and ask God's forgiveness. We acknowledge our struggles and we ask for strength to serve Him in newness of life.

We are by now about five minutes into the service, and it is to be hoped that we will be able to survive that long without any mortal sin! The important thing is not the prayer itself but the content we bring to it: our thoughts, our feelings of penitence, the loads we carry which we ask Christ to bear with us, and from which we want Him to help us free ourselves. God, we are sinners, help us! We need to believe that He will forgive us.

The Priest or President pronounces **the absolution**, sometimes by making the sign of the cross over the whole congregation, sometimes by simply holding up a hand, at others by just standing and reading the words. Whatever way it is done, it is indeed a powerful act. Here the Priest, with all the authority of Christ Himself, pronounces God's forgiveness to all who truly repent. On many occasions a cold shudder goes down my spine when I present this. The absolution is a call to true repentance and a deliverance from the sins which we so often cling to, and we are to be strengthened and confirmed in goodness and eternal life, for that is what we are looking for, through Christ.

We are now primed with a confidence, and rightly

so, to move forward a little closer to the reception of the sacrament.

There are a couple of things that we can do beforehand. One is the recitation of the **Kyrie Eleison**, usually used in Lent and Advent for their penitential overtones. The other is the **Gloria in Excelsis**, where we call upon and glorify in high praise Jesus the Son of God, acknowledging His oneness with God. Jesus, the one who takes away the sins of the world and through whom we find salvation. It does give the service a lift after all that penitence! The *Gloria* is of course much older than the Alternative Service book, and is indeed a hymn of praise to God.

The next section of our service takes us to the heading **The Ministry of the Word**. We hear and read the Collect, Old Testament Lesson, Epistle and Gospel for the day, all carefully chosen by the compilers to be linked in some way and making relevant their use in the service. We will not dwell here on these readings, usually called The Lectionary, as we are concentrating on the Prayers used in the Eucharist. The sermon is usually reserved for the main service of the day, although I did pop my head around a church door on a Sunday recently and heard a sermon, not really my cup of tea at 8.00 in the morning. I slipped out again and said my prayers at home.

The Nicene Creed follows the sermon and is a statement of Christian belief dating from the first Council of Nicea in the fourth century. It is a clear statement of what Christian believe, and can often be held in reserve when challenged by someone as to what we do believe. It divides very nicely into four sections. First,

> We believe in one God,
> the Father, the Almighty,
> maker of heaven and earth,
> of all that is,
> seen and unseen.

This says a lot about orthodox belief in God the Creator of the Universe, at the top of the pyramid so to speak, responsible Creator of all things. Quite frankly a very simple concept to state but perhaps more difficult for twentieth-century man to understand.

Immediately we have sorted out our belief in God we turn to Jesus:

> We believe in one Lord, Jesus Christ,
> the only Son of God,
> eternally begotten of the Father,
> God from God, Light from Light,
> true God from true God,
> begotten, not made,
> of one being with the Father.

Here the compilers of the truths held in the Nicene creed wrestle with the problem of making God and Jesus one. "Begotten not made" – God and Jesus here are one, and that is the point being made, that God was in Christ... of one being with the Father.

Jesus is not another part of God, He is God.

> Through Him all things were made.

We are reminded of God the Creator of all things. The story now moves on to the birth of Christ and we are told immediately why He came from heaven.

> For us men and for us salvation He came
> down from heaven;

God in Christ came down from heaven to save mankind, this special part of His creation, and the way He did it was

> By the power of the Holy Spirit He
> became incarnate of the Virgin Mary
> and was made man.

In a few short sentences we have moved with God to Jesus and now to the Holy Spirit!, let alone the Virgin Mary, the first earthly link with mankind and Jesus. Once again, for the minds of the time these concepts were acceptable, and to tell you the truth I find them very acceptable myself without too much complicated study. God simply took a hand in the affairs of mankind, and in Jesus Christ became a man. To make it more credible that mankind could be saved, Jesus had to be seen to be human, and so He was born just like any other man and had a mother whose name was Mary. How He was conceived I have never found a stumbling block to faith. That is for the power of God to do and not for me to reason over. It is a mystery, and all the speculation will not strengthen my faith. The simple truth embodied in the creed tells us that God in Christ Jesus came into the world and Mary was a channel of that grace. Neither would I wish to diminish any scholarship or learning which asks any searching questions, the simple truth being that we shall never know. But this is what I believe and that will always have to be a matter of faith. Our story moves on:

> For our sake He was crucified under
>   Pontius Pilate; He suffered death and
>   was buried.

Once again a simple statement of truth and made factual by the historic reference to Pontius Pilate. Jesus died and was buried.

> On the third day He rose again
> in accordance with the Scriptures;
> He ascended into heaven and is seated at
>   the right hand of the Father.

Quite simply, as you turn the page in the service book you come across the earth-shattering statement that Jesus rose from the dead, just as the Scriptures said he would, and then ascended into heaven to sit at the right hand of the Father. It would be rather inconvenient to have Jesus wandering around the earth having risen from the dead, because then faith would be out and we would be compelled to believe in God, thereby losing the free choice which God has given to mankind. That is why we have the ascension, the going up of Jesus into heaven.

Next we have a statement about the second coming of Christ:

> He will come again in glory to judge the
> living and the dead, and His kingdom
> will have no end.

The second coming of Christ has caused much speculation, and I am not really sure what it is supposed to be. Perhaps it will be a final sorting out or something when the world or I come to an end. It is a subject of much speculation but points to some form of Judgement, about which religious people are very keen. Is it because they look for some reward above others? I am not quite sure about this one.

The section about Jesus comes to an end with Him safely tucked up in heaven, with a threat, or a promise, to return again. In the meantime we turn our attention to the Holy Spirit. This is certainly a mystical figure and concept. I think it was John Austin Baker in his book *The Foolishness of God* who described the Holy Spirit as "The presence of Jesus in His absence".

> We believe in the Holy Spirit,
> the Lord, the giver of life,
> who proceeds from the Father and the
> Son.

> With the Father and the Son He is
> worshipped and glorified.

The Holy Spirit is at one with God and Jesus, and proceeds from them into the world, and we must hold the Holy Spirit as one with them both. The third member of the Trinity as this joyous threesome have come to be known. Not only that but

> He has spoken through the prophets.

This links the Holy Spirit with the prophets of old, so it was probably He who, through the prophets, foretold the coming of Jesus.

We leave the heavenly sections and return to mankind and the apostolic Church, founded by Jesus and settled by His apostles as an instrument of His grace.

> We believe in one holy catholic and
> apostolic church.

Here we express what we believe the Church to be. When we say "catholic" in this sense we mean universal (it is not linked solely to the Roman Church), a church that covers the world.

> We acknowledge one baptism for the
> forgiveness of sins.

The Church carries out the orders of Jesus to baptize men everywhere for the forgiveness of sins.

We look for the resurrection of the dead,
and the life of the world to come.
Amen.

This is our expression of Christian hope for the future.

The Nicene has it all there for us to ponder upon, and as an aid to prayer we can meditate quite easily on the occasional phrase from this work. In the context of the public communion service it is so often glossed over and seen as something that takes a while to be said, so we say it as quickly and as loudly as we can. I like to listen to what I am saying, what I am agreeing to, even when reciting the creed in public, and I really do not want to hear what my neighbour is saying or the way he is saying it. I am affirming my belief, with all the questions that I have in God.

The next section in the book is labelled **The Intercession**. As this is a book about prayer and I have already written about interceding, I intend to write little here other than to ask a couple of questions. Why is it so difficult to find people to lead the prayers in church? Is it because we make them feel that there is a them-and-us atmosphere? ''The priest is here so he must do it.'' Sadly those who often push themselves forward are those who are least able to do it, whereas those who hold back are often ideal. It is the community who intercedes in public worship and not just the priest. True, we do add our own intercession to those of the leader but we are together praying to God. Don't overload these prayers, give space and silence a chance.

When I do visit a strange parish to take a service I always ask for someone in the community to take the prayers, as hopefully they will have more of an idea of what is going on and should know some of the issues relevant to that community.

We turn two pages in the Alternative Service Book and come to the prayer at the top of page 128, which I always know as **the Prayer of Humble Access**. It is for me one of the most noble prayers retained in the new service, neither grovelling or chichi. It points us to the Eucharist and our communion with God, and we move forward as a community on pilgrimage.

> We do not presume
> to come to this your table, merciful Lord,
> trusting in our own righteousness,
> but in your manifold and great mercies.
> We are not worthy
> so much as to gather up the crumbs
>   under
> your table.
> But you are the same Lord
> whose nature is always to have mercy.
> Grant us therefore, gracious Lord,
> so to eat the flesh of Your dear Son
> Jesus Christ
> and to drink His blood,
> that we may ever more dwell in Him
> and He in us. Amen.

This prayer I always prefer to say on my knees. We are approaching God's table asking for a deeper communion with Him. I have always believed that table fellowship is very important, and this has been reflected through the centuries, with food being a part of many religious festivals of all kinds and marking the many celebratory points of our lives, both happy and sad. Here we continue to move towards entering into a deeper fellowship with God. Perhaps today, sadly, we do not place enough emphasis in our social life on table fellowship, and therefore some of the power of this prayer loses out. We acknowledge in this prayer that we rely entirely on God's goodness and not any of our own, knowing that God is merciful, and we ask to enter into His fellowship of the table, and more than that to dwell in Him as He surely dwells with us.

We move on to one of the most controversial parts of the service, **The Peace!** Oh dear! the number of arguments I have heard for and against this activity in the service. We are actually encouraged to get up and at least shake hands with our neighbours, whom we may not even know, let alone like! In different parts of the country and the world there are different reactions to touching a stranger in a semi-formal or formal way. Let's face it: the majority of British people are not great touchers. This may be because we are an island race, and we also have respect for other people's privacy. Rightly used however the **Peace** can be a powerful prayer. It signifies acceptance of the other person, as God accepts us all. I have used it to good effect when I have had a strong disagreement with a parishioner (oh yes, we clergy don't always like every parishioner). In the formality of the service the Peace has been used to heal our differences and open up a respect for one another. I notice among the elderly, especially those who have lost their partners, there is a willingness to shake hands and communicate this way in the peace. Sensitively done and not rushed or delayed overlong, it can have a striking effect in the service, people seem to relax after it and it does build up fellowship. It is a living prayer and one I look forward to.

The Peace gives way to **The Preparation of the Gifts** and the **Eucharistic Prayer**. The Preparation of the Gifts can be as simple as taking the bread and wine to the altar, and sometimes this is done with great ceremonial. But I like simplicity. I have always tried to introduce the system of a welcoming person at the door of the church as people come in, and inviting them to place their bread from a plate into the vessel which takes the bread to the altar. Everyone who comes into church symbolically places a little of themselves, their hopes and fears, in with the bread, and all these from the whole community are brought up to the altar at this point in the vessel containing them. A little symbolism which falls flat on some! However we arrive at the **Eucharistic Prayer.** In fact in the Alternative Service Book there are four Eucharistic Prayers. For the lay man this is confusing enough, but it is an attempt by the committee to try to write a Eucharistic Prayer which the many groups within the Church can use. I will simply look at the one I have used most often, The First Eucharistic Prayer.

We are working to the climax of the Eucharist or

Holy Communion, and one of the most controversial points: the moment of consecration. In the main the largest part of the prayer is presented by the President or Priest, but I have been to services where this has been split up and shared with a deacon or other licensed person.

We begin with a greeting and a call to give thanks to the Lord our God. The priest continues:

> It is indeed right,
> it is our duty and our joy,
> at all times and in all places
> to give you thanks and praise,
> holy Father, heavenly King,
> almighty and eternal God,
> through Jesus Christ your only Son our
>   Lord.

For me this section points once again to the universality of God, reminding us of His presence everywhere, and therefore in all aspects of our lives as we strive to give Him glory, and we do this by following the ways of Christ.

> For he is Your living Word;
> through Him you have created all things
>   from the beginning,
> and formed us in Your own image.

The pen being mightier than the sword is a maxim confirmed by the power of the Word of God, written once in the Old Testament and now confirmed and brought to life in Christ. Once again we are reminded of God the Creator, and our being made in His image is something we often undervalue.

> Through Him You have freed us from
>   the slavery of sin,
> giving Him to be born as man and to die
>   upon the Cross;
> You raised Him from the dead
> and exalted Him to Your right hand on
>   high.
> Through Him You have sent upon us
> Your holy and life-giving Spirit,
> and made us a people for Your own
>   possession.

Here we recall some of those events in Christ's life confirmed in the creeds, and we are told that it is through Christ's death and resurrection that we are freed from our sins or the slavery of sin. The Ascension is recalled, and the sending of the Holy Spirit, and a comforting word that we are His people, the people of God.

There follows a section where we can include a proper preface which continues the theme of the service.

> Therefore with angels and archangels,
> and with all the company of heaven,

> we proclaim Your great and glorious
>   name,
> for ever praising You and saying;

ALL:

> Holy, holy, holy, Lord,
> God of power and might,
> heaven and earth are full of Your glory,
> Hosanna in the highest.
>
> Blessed is He who comes in the name of
>   the Lord.
> Hosanna in the highest!

We all recite this exaltation, lifting our thoughts to the glory of dwelling with God in heaven and acknowledging the heavenly host. We are lifted from this world into the life beyond, with echoes of the second coming.

The President continues with the Eucharistic Prayer:

> Accept our praises, heavenly Father,
> through Your Son our Saviour Jesus
>   Christ;
> and as we follow His example and obey
>   His command,
> grant that by the power of Your Holy
>   Spirit

these gifts of bread and wine
may be to us His body and His blood.

I always like to pause a little after this section. There is so much to take in. We are asking God to accept the life that we offer, our life, as we struggle to follow Jesus's example and try to obey His rule of love. We are entering into a deeper fellowship with Christ and asking for a strengthening. We are calling upon the Holy Spirit to help us enter the life of Christ by sharing of the bread and wine. A time for strengthening.

We continue:

Who in the same night that He was
  betrayed,
took bread and gave You thanks;
He broke it and gave it to His disciples,
saying,
"Take, eat; this is My body which is
  given for you;
do this in remembrance of Me."
In the same way, after supper
He took the cup and gave You thanks;
He gave it to them, saying,
"Drink this, all of you;
this is My blood of the new covenant,
which is shed for you and for many for
  the forgiveness of sins.

> Do this as often as you drink it,
> in remembrance of Me."

We recall that moment at the Last Supper when Jesus ate with His disciples and shared the bread with them, symbolically His body, of which we are all a part as a member of the Church, a body which will be broken on the Cross, in suffering. He goes on to offer the cup, the wine, the new life blood, His blood, which is to be shed. It is shed though for a reason: for the forgiveness of our sins. Yes, man destroys the life of the Son of God on the Cross but God forgives mankind that by raising Jesus from the dead. Here is the sign that despite all our human failings and weakness, and all the so-called power that we have in this world, it is God who is the real power, who has the power of life and death, and as He gives life back to Jesus, so too by entering into fellowship with Him we may have life and that life will be eternal. Our sins will be forgiven and we are part of His body. It is a moment of great solemnity.

We then all proclaim the threefold acclamation of our faith:

> Christ has died:
> Christ is risen;
> Christ will come again.

The President continues:

> Therefore, heavenly Father,
> we remember His offering of Himself

made once for all upon the Cross,
and proclaim His mighty resurrection
   and glorious Ascension.
As we look for His coming in glory,
we celebrate with this bread and this cup
His one perfect sacrifice.

The old ways of offering sacrifices to God, of animals
and the like, were never necessary and are now made
totally obsolete. That is not the way and never was.
Jesus has offered Himself on the Cross, taking with
Him our human lot, and God has raised Him from
the dead, thus breaking the bonds of death. The
mighty act of redeeming mankind has taken place,
we are shown the way and we must respond.

Accept through Him, our great high
   priest,
this our sacrifice of thanks and praise;
and as we eat and drink these holy gifts
in the presence of Your divine majesty,
renew us by Your Spirit,
inspire us with Your love,
and unite us in the body of Your Son,
Jesus Christ, our Lord.

Jesus becomes the great high priest, and we ask God
to accept our simple sacrifice of praise and
thanksgiving through this sacrament and the lives we
offer, our lives, to be lived to His praise and glory.

We celebrate the presence of the divine majesty of God at this second and always, now heightened by this holy moment. We ask for renewal as we commit our lives at this time, by the power of the presence of Jesus in His absence, the Holy Spirit. This is not enough. We ask to be inspired by the love that God has shown, and that we may show that love in the world, and we ask for unity within the family of faith, the body of Christ.

> Through Him, and with Him and in
>   Him, by the power of the Holy Spirit,
> with all who stand before You in earth
>   and heaven,
> we worship You, Father almighty,
> in songs of everlasting praise:
>
> Blessing and honour and glory and power
> be Yours for ever and ever. Amen.

So we end with an exaltation acknowledging that it is through Jesus that we are able to offer our incomplete and imperfect lives to God, as we seek to bring ourselves to His Kingdom. Then we settle for a silence, a time to reflect upon our own thoughts, about what has been recalled and what has gone on before.

The Lord's Prayer follows, then we come to what is known as **The Fraction**. This is the moment when the priest breaks the bread.

> We break this bread
> to share in the body of Christ.
> Though we are many, we are one body,
> because we all share in one bread.

Here the priest takes the bread and breaks it, ready
for sharing with the people, symbolizing the sharing
of the body of Christ and acknowledging the unity of
the many.
A choice of **two short anthems** follows, and then the
priest invites the people to come forward and receive
the bread and wine.

> Draw near with faith. Receive the body
> of our Lord Jesus Christ which He
> gave for you, and His blood which He
> shed for you.

> Eat and drink in remembrance that He
> died for you, and feed on Him in your
> hearts by faith with thanksgiving.

The words of invitation speak of Faith, not
knowledge. They invite us to move towards God and
receive this symbolic communion with Him. We
have to make a move in response to God's invitation,
and we move forward.

For me this is one of the most meaningful parts of
the whole service. The administration can take place
in different ways. If there is a very large congregation
there may be three or four places in the church where

people are invited to go and receive the Sacrament. If there are not too many, then most come forward to the altar rail and kneel, and cross their hands waiting to receive the elements of the communion. I always like to look at the hands of those who come. They all tell a story. Children's hands, women's hands, smooth hands of office workers, and hard, horny hands of those who earn their living by hard physical work. No matter who, rich or poor, they all come and seek to receive God's grace. The elements are usually offered with a few words of administration:

The Body of Christ.

The Blood of Christ.

It is traditional for you to remain kneeling until your neighbour has received, and then move off back to your place in the main congregation.

After the administration there are a choice of prayers. The one I prefer to use is:

Almighty God,
we thank You for feeding us
with the body and blood of Your Son
Jesus Christ.
Through Him we offer You our souls and
bodies
to be a living sacrifice.
Send us out
in the power of Your Spirit

> to live and work
> to Your praise and glory. Amen.

I like this prayer as it sums up so much of what I feel we have been through. We offer thanks to God for the communion, and we remind ourselves that we too are offering something, our souls and bodies to be a living sacrifice, not wrapped up and protected from life, but involved and living as a sacrifice of service to God for the good of all. We call upon the Holy Spirit to give us power to live and work for the glory of God.

The service closes with a **blessing**.

The prayers in the communion service are often so familiar that they lose their impact. It is so important to think as we pray these words and to listen with care. Not all the prayers will speak to us all the time, but there will be those occasions when a note strikes and we are brought up with a start, a moment of recognition, of challenge.

As a whole it is a prayer in itself involving action and commitment in which we are involved. No matter how we dress it with beautiful music and ceremony, it is basically a very simple and humbling act when we come and prepare ourselves, by leaving our sins at the foot of the Cross and move forward to receive communion and then, strengthened, go out into the world to serve.

8

Penitence

The first confession I made to a priest was unprepared and in many way spontaneous, although I was burdened down with guilt. It happened in the RAF Church in Fleet Street. My business affairs were in a state, and in some ways I wanted to make a deal with God. Deep down I knew there was no deal to be made, but I needed to make some confession...

Each new day is born of a certain innocence as the sun rises and the fresh air wakes a sleeping countryside. There is a freshness and a silence with just the bird song adding sweetness to the morning. It does not take long, however, for this stillness and innocence to change, as the countryside begins to wake up and the roads begin to fill and another working day begins to take its toll on the peace that once was. The innocence is somehow spoilt and the day tarnished. We all have to accept that somewhere along the line we have to face some guilt for one act or another, and if we face the fact of guilt then perhaps it makes it easier for us to look for penitence – both uncomfortable words and subjects. Some people say that Christianity is a guilt-ridden religion, at least in the Church of England. Not only do we seem trapped in it, but in a perverse way we seem to want to be trapped in it, holding our heads down low and being thoroughly miserable because of our imperfections, revelling in our own misery. This surely, if it were true, must be an unhealthy attitude.

Looking at some of the written services used by the Church over the years there does seem in some to be an unhealthy bias towards the penitential side of things for us "miserable sinners"! First we have to look and think about what actually is a sin. I remember once being told that it is anything that separates us from God, anything that gets in the way of focusing on Christ.

There is no doubt that when we do something wrong, and we know it is wrong, it does seem to fill our thoughts, as we cannot put it out of our minds, to the cost of thinking about anything else. We have a sort of block on thinking about other things, and our judgement in other things is clouded until we can be relieved of the burden which is troubling us. This is guilt and we need to be rid of it for our own spiritual, mental and sometimes physical health.

The treatment of guilt may need to be helped by a specialist, and so we may go to the priest if we are a strong believer, or sometimes to the doctor or psychiatrist or faith healer. All these channels have been used by believers and non-believers alike. Some forms of guilt isolate people, and they then need to be brought back into circulation in order to help them see that forgiveness can be theirs. Many people write to the agony aunts in newspapers or on radio or television through a sense of guilt, wanting some form of recognition and acceptance, as they see that telling these people about their problems is a form of confession.

We do need a gentle hand with ourselves when we

begin to look at the question of guilt and forgiveness
for the first time. There is within most of us, since the
Fall of Adam and Eve, a sense of guilt. Used
sensitively it can bring guidance and health if we
learn and understand the signals that our sense of
guilt presents to us. A sense of guilt needs some
relief, and this in turn sometimes means that we need
to be penitent. At other times we may be feeling
guilty when there is no reason at all. In both cases it
helps to discuss the problem with someone if you feel
you cannot rationalize it yourself and accept
responsibility, or not, for your guilt. The most
difficult thing, though, is to learn that you can be
forgiven, and then how to accept forgiveness.

Let us look at an extreme case. A serious crime is
committed. The person who did the crime is
arrested, tried and convicted. There is no doubt that
he is guilty and he is given a prison sentence.
While awaiting trial he sees his priest and repents
earnestly. Most people believe that his penitence is
genuine, so does the judge, but he is still sent to
prison for a term. What do we make of this?

For the truly penitent the forgiveness of God is
given freely to all who sincerely repent.
Unfortunately we are weaker than God, we cannot
see into men's hearts, and we need to mete out some
punishment. When the punishment has been
administered or served, then we need to be able to
welcome the person back into society and support
them. This is in an ideal world.

The story of the Prodigal Son reflects God's free
forgiveness as the father welcomes the boy home
after squandering his inheritance, the boy having

repented and admitted his guilt. Society needs protecting, and a point needs to be made, so usually there is a punishment given.

There are many things which trouble us in the course of our lives, and we need to find some relief from them. The General Confession in the Prayer Book can be used to great effect, and does generally seem to be recited more thoughtfully than a good number of the prayers that we say together. How do we prepare for this act of confession? Well, I dare say that a good number of us do not prepare half as carefully as we ought to. Personal examination is something we need to work at, but not to make a burden for ourselves that we cannot support. In a simple way there may well be things for which during the week we are sorry, and if we cannot make amends because the moment has passed, then why not simply bring them to mind during the General Confession and then LET GO of them. The angry word, the fit of bad temper, the bad mood – confess them and then leave them at the foot of the Cross. Remember you are human and are not the only one who has bad thoughts and bad moments. But if you are fortunate enough to recongize the fact, admit it, confess it – and then let it go and try harder next time! Do not be trapped by your humanity, accept God's forgiveness in our frailty. Remember, Jesus knows what it is to be human, and if we are penitent then forgiveness comes freely flowing. We have to learn, though, to accept it.

There are times in one's life when perhaps the General Confession may not be enough, when more specialized counselling is needed. Immediately the picture springs to mind of those dark confessionals we see in continental churches, with a priest separated from the penitent by a gauze screen and the words, ''Forgive me Father for I have sinned...'' For those practised in this art, it is no bad thing. For those looking at confession and penitence seriously for the first time, it may well put you off for life if you feel that it has to be this way.

To a priest in his own parish the anonymity that the confessional affords is a good thing, although in small parishes it must be difficult for him not to recognize the odd voice. If you feel that you need this form of confession then it is not unknown, and indeed in some cases is considered wise, to ask your parish priest to point you in the direction of some other priest whom you do not know to make your confession to. You can talk to your priest about the technicalities without making any mention of the need for your confession. Careful preparation is necessary if you really are going to make good use of the occasion. You do need to know what you are being penitent about. This may sound rather strange, but often the first thing that presents itself need not be the real cause of your need of penitence and forgiveness. A simple discussion can often help. Those things that deeply disturb you about yourself may need specialized help, but if it is a question of your relationship with God then the priest is the one charged to absolve your sin.

Today many people find it necessary to find a friend or a counsellor with whom they can be completely open, and this in itself can be a healing form of confession. For that is what confession is: a

restoration and a healing, though it does need to be
able to find some form of acceptance of forgiveness in
the person concerned.

I look back to a time in my life when things were
not going too well. As a young man full of ambition I
had got myself in a tight corner. My work was
mainly in London, and things were going seriously
wrong. I was taking too many chances, and now it
looked as though all I had worked for was about to
collapse. One day I was in the Strand and went into a
church. It was fairly early in the day and there was a
priest there hearing some confessions. He had
obviously had rather a large number of people for he
looked very tired. I waited until he was free and went
and knelt. I cannot remember what I said, or indeed
if I was particularly honest in the confession I made.
In fact I was ill prepared. He listened patiently and I
remember what he said: "Be generous". That was
all. I was a little taken aback as I had expected
slightly more guidance, but I had not been altogether
clear to him. On reflection, however, he had hit the
nail on the head. I was caught up with my own self
and was not really thinking about the consequences
of my actions or life on other people. I needed to look
at how my actions were likely to affect other people,
and to find ways not only of being generous to them
but also to myself, to forgive my mistakes. It was not
a dramatic turning point, but it was one which came
to take effect slowly as I realized the implications of
what he had said.

Others find it helpful to go on retreat from time to
time, and to stay at a quiet place while they think
about their lives. Retreats can be led with a group or

designed for the individual. At the end of a retreat some people make their confession to the resident priest and go on their way, strengthened, to face the world, and having found themselves again.

The counselling session today often acts as a form of confession for many people, either with the priest or a trained counsellor, for no matter who we discuss or what problems we have, it is we who have to find and accept that forgiveness which is so readily given. It may mean a dramatic change in one's life, or simply an adjustment to some undiscovered fact about oneself, and then some building on controlling that area.

There is no doubt in my mind that we all need to use prayer to help us keep focus on the way we are, offering to God those things about ourselves which we wish to change and learning to accept what we are. There are times when we are caught in a crisis, and a situation which we know is wrong, and the temptation is to turn our back on prayer, but this is folly. We need to face our lives squarely as they are and to measure them against the way that Christ has tried to show. In our darkest moments we can and should continue to ask God to help us.

It is quite a natural feeling that when we are penitent we feel unclean and as though the world is watching us. We need to be washed in God's forgiving balm. We will also need resolve to change and to put right those etchings which we can. It is part of the ministry of the church community as a whole to work at God's forgiveness and to restore people to His glory.

The Penitential seasons of the Church, Lent and

Advent, are useful reminders of the need to look at our lives and to reassess where we are going and what life is all about, to be self-examining and honest with ourselves. To be honest with ourselves too when we know that we feel penitent and need forgiveness, and to be honest with ourselves when we feel we have received it.

9

Freedom

With the ever expanding achievements of mankind it has become increasingly difficult for us to give up that sense and quest for freedom that our dependence upon God the Creator defines. We can turn our backs on God and pretend He does not exist. But we cannot escape the ultimate reality of death, and perhaps when dying the most ardent atheist has been known to be a little uncertain about the existence of a God.

Working with those who have a very limited life span, either as a helper in a hospice, or in the hospital where I was an operating theatre technician, or as a parish priest, calls for a very special kind of honesty about God. "I do not *know* but I believe, I live by faith", was often part of the conversation I would have with people, and I always asked, "What about you, what do you think?" Many were so glad to have the chance, often for the first time in their lives, to speak about what they really felt about God, and how they had used prayer in their lives.

There is a saying, "Man is free, but everywhere he is in chains". No matter how hard we try, we are having to live under limitations of society, laws and our own abilities. We all know the limitations shortage of money and other restraints can bring. Yet despite many limitations, the human spirit does aspire and does achieve some amazing goals. We only have to look at the spirited disabled people in our communities to see the human spirit towering over all difficulties. In my last parish there was a chap in a wheelchair who was always putting us to shame by his abilities in the field of wheelchair sports. There was an old lady crippled with arthritis, who insisted on keeping her own home, despite all our well-meaning efforts to have her rehoused. She valued her independence.

There are strange paradoxes too. I used to visit a prison quite regularly, and it was amazing to see some of the works of art, of great beauty, produced by some inmates who had perpetrated terrible crimes. Trapped as they were by their weaknesses, they were yet able to find some form of freedom in expressing themselves through their art.

Living as we do with some kinds of constraint, we long to be free. Most of us, as we grow older, adjust to the fact that what we were once able to do as young people we find increasingly difficult as age creeps on, and so we seek other ways of freedom and expression.

When it comes to our faith and search for God we are in this country free to find what ways we will. There is no persecution of religion. Again we have another paradox, for where there has been persecution it would seem that the faith of those who have been persecuted has been strong and strengthened, and they have survived in some form or another. An old friend of mine who worked in China as a priest before the Second World War, tells a story of an area where the authorities were worried about the growth of Christianity, and some sections of the ruling order sought to persecute the Christians out of existence. Yet despite persecution – or perhaps because of it? – Christianity survived. Those who had worked at the skill through their lives, despite sometimes tragic circumstances, through efforts at prayer had found a freedom that offered space from their immediate misery and insight into God. A wise elder of the community insisted that they should be left alone, for he declared that if they were persecuted they would flourish. I never discovered what the outcome was.

For all the restrictions upon us in this life we can use prayer to help find a freedom. It will not be a freedom that relieves us of responsibility for our actions and responses to the authorities of this life, but a deeper freedom that enables us to work within the society in which we live. It should not be seen as an escape to a fantasy world, but to a greater reality. I am not sure that my analogies will work, but I will try to explain as best I can.

Through learning about and actually praying we acknowledge the existence of some force, some activity, greater than ourselves, which somehow is the ultimate authority. This authority we call God, and Christians believe Him to be a God of Love, of all that is good. He calls us to Himself, and we have the free will to respond by taking up the journey or to deny Him. Despite all our failings, and as imperfect as we may be, to a lesser or greater degree, He will not turn us away if we seek His will, repent of our sins and ask for His help. We are called to be faithful to the journey, not necessarily successful. We try to

communicate with Him through prayer, and this is
not a way of getting from God what we want but a
way of getting what He wants from us. God does not
need to make up His mind, but we need to make up
our own, and prayer helps us in this. One of the
great sadnesses is that we so easily give up on prayer,
or lose sight of the relevance of it, when we do not
seem to be getting the responses that we want!

We do need to look at ourselves and discover what
we are and how we lead our lives. My work in a
hospital and in a hospice has been a great help to me
in working a few things out. The body is definitely
mortal, and if I did not fully accept that before I
worked in a hospital I certainly did after working
there for a short time. The machine, which, no
matter how complex, is what the body is, and the
care of it, takes up a good deal of our lives, but it is a
machine with a dimension like no other. It has a life
and existence like no other animal machine: a sense
of reason and a mind to use, and in some respects
these elements have limitations imposed on them by
the body in which they dwell. But the mind has the
ability to reason and think about things outside the
body, and that is why so much is achieved by
mankind, despite their physical limitations. Some
people are able to use this ability in artistic ways –
painting, writing and others – in sheer determination
to put the physical through seemingly impossible
feats. There is also the ability to discover the paths of
prayer which have no limitations, and indeed can
help us find enormous freedom when they help us
accept some of the limitations and restrictions of this
mortal life.

When I went to work in the hospice I was not really sure what I was letting myself in for. I was simply to be an unpaid helper for a few weeks. Much to my surprise I found it quite a jolly place. Not in the sense of the frivolous, but of real joy. Many people who came for treatment were there for pain control, others were really in the terminal stages of illness and needed support until death came, as their needs were greater than home could supply.

We never told people that they were dying. They would often question and hint at wanting us to confirm what they knew deep within themselves, but it was up to them, and I believe rightly so, to ask the question outright. One lady I was looking after, although by then free of pain, was deeply troubled and had that troubled look on her face. Over the weeks we got to know each other quite well and built up confidences. She knew that I was training to be a priest, but she had never shown any interest in joining in some of the ward services that were held on a regular basis. One day, quite out of the blue, she asked to see me. Her question was direct: "Am I dying?" I think she expected me to answer yes or no, but my training had been such that I put the question back to her, "What do you think?" "Well, I think I am." "How do you feel about it?" There was a silence for a while, and I held her hand, "Quite relieved actually". Over the next few days, even though she became weaker her face seemed to grow younger and less strained, and she joined in the ward services. The truth was that this lady had always said her prayers, as I later discovered. She told how for years, despite the many difficulties of her life, she had found a freedom in praying that she had not found elsewhere. Then why her nervousness about joining in the ward prayers? She was frightened of losing the freedom her prayer life had given her, just in case she did not feel the same afterwards, after accepting that she was dying. To her joy she had found confirmation of that freedom she had experienced through prayer. She was not through her prayers escaping into a fantasy world as she had feared, but she had found and faced a reality, and that reality did not disappear when she had come to accept the ultimate truth that she was about to experience. It need not be the same for everyone.

There is a danger that investing in prayer can lead to fantasy, and we can be trapped by these fantasies rather than living in reality, a reality which accepts our own human failings and frailty and utter dependence on the mercy of God. We can be carried on a tide of emotion and live in a flighty world of fantasy, not finding the real strength to tackle problems we actually find in ourselves. These dangers really exist if we insist upon praying in isolation and not exposing our thoughts and prayers to others, and indeed not necessarily those with whom we always agree. This isolationism can exist with a community of faith as well as an individual. Like-minded people do need to look outside the security of their own ideas to see how others pray and express their beliefs in God. The ecumenical movement has done a great deal to help us all face this challenge.

The acceptance that others, while holding to orthodox Christian beliefs, can express their prayers in ways other than our own strengthens the whole community.

There is an aspect of prayer which is often overlooked. It can be a very private and personal event. There is no physical action necessary to prayer, and there is no need to make much noise. Indeed, all the praying that needs to be done can be done in the silence of the mind. Only God and yourself will know the nature of your prayers. This gives a wonderful chance of being free with God, to bring before Him all those things for which you are glad and those things for which you need special support and help.

I do have a feeling that we are somewhat split personalities, in as much as when we are prying secretly perhaps we are addressing our prayers to some matter or another, but underneath there is the real reason for our prayer, God sees this and responds to it rather than to that which we put first in our minds, perhaps not aware of this hidden prayer ourselves.

The great thing is that you can be completely free to be secret in your prayers, no matter what your physical conditions and surroundings may be. This means that if you have the courage you can take a long look at yourself and be completely honest about how you see yourself and the way you lead your life. When it was suggested that I might be considered for the ministry I spent some time in a little simple self-analysis. I wrote down on two sheets of paper all the bad things I felt I was, and then on another sheet all the good qualities I thought I had. Not surprisingly, all the bad things took up more space than all the good things, of which there seemed very few. On reflection I still consider this to have been a useful exercise, but now I would seek more help in creating a better balance, sharing with God those things which really troubled me.

At times it is not enough just to share things with God, but a spiritual director or other person may be necessary. We all need a little counselling from time to time. Unfortunately, counselling seems to carry with it a bit of a stigma, and this in the Christian sense is most unfair. It is good to have someone objective to talk things over with, to help you see how perhaps God may be responding to your requests. It is helpful sometimes for someone to point you in the direction of the right answers, or to have them share their experience of similar circumstances and situations in which you may find yourself. The need for this sort of support can often come from someone older to whom you may relate. It is also wise to remember that as you get older it becomes increasingly difficult to find even older people to help you! The need though may remain the same.

It is a question of finding a soul friend with whom you can be as honest as your secret prayers. and in whom you can trust. You must not always expect them to be sympathetic, and they may exercise some form of judgement to help stimulate your thinking. This kind of honesty in prayer can bring a feeling of enormous relief, often for many reasons. The fact that someone else listens to you and responds and accepts you as you are does help you find a freedom to continue on your journey of prayer. It is a form of confirmation that what you are doing is acceptable, and it is always good to know that others feel the same.

In discovering the freedom in prayer and being honest in dealing with this opportunity it is a way of helping cope with some of the difficult situations in which you can find yourself in life. It can act as a window, albeit a window of faith, into the experience of heaven. I have no idea what heaven will be like. I have a friend who is a monk at the Abbey of Bec in Normandy, who is convinced that heaven is a vast church with choir stalls set out in collegiate fashion, with monks on one side and nuns on the other, singing the psalms continuously. In this thought he finds great freedom. For myself I really hope and pray it will not be like that.

The freedom that prayer brings is one to communicate in complete confidence with God. It is to lift oneself from this world to an acknowledgement of that greater reality which forms a part of the creation which we so often ignore. Our sense of freedom comes from continually being aware that although in this world, and subject to the many forces within it, in prayer we can link with the creative activity through which all creation receives its power, and that in Christ this activity is for the good of all. It is not so much an escape as a meeting with reality and truth.

When we find truth and face it we also find freedom. The truth is that we can pray to God our Creator and know that we are heard and that our inarticulate utterings are understood. We may not receive the answer clearly, or in the way we would wish, but we can be assured that our prayer is not wasted. We must not look for results and clear answers, but develop the freedom to pray and let go, so that God in His way will help us see the results of our prayers and give us the strength and the freedom to go. We need not go on to be successful people, but we have the freedom to be faithful people.

10

Praying with the Dying

When I was first a curate there was that embarrassing moment when I was in someone's home soon after a relative had died. The undertaker had done the usual thing, taken the body away, and then telephoned the Vicar or whoever he could get hold of. The family stricken with grief are sitting there on the edge of their seats, and here is the Vicar person only usually seen at baptisms, weddings and funerals. Despite their lack of interest in the Church you know you are welcome and they want you there. The question is, do I say a prayer or don't I? It can be very difficult to judge. Some people are affronted by the idea in their anger. After all, in some eyes it is God who has caused all this grief. Others just don't want to know and are embarrassed by the idea. Then there are those who breathe a sigh of relief, thinking that you were never going to ask. "Would you like me to say a prayer?" The question I have posed often has never been refused.

Naturally it is difficult to know what to say, especially if you have never known the personality of the person who has died. It is a great mistake to take too much for granted, and often in these cases it is better to stick to the abstract, praying not only for the deceased but for those who remain as well. If you are doing an off the cuff prayer then keep it simple, uncomplicated and free from too much religious and flowery language. Be natural and try to do what comes naturally. I give you a simple example:

> God our Father,
> take to your safe keeping
> the soul of ....
> Grant him peace and share that peace
> with those who now suffer his loss.
> Amen.

You do not need to go on at great length, and the sense of relief once you have opened the door of prayer will be great. Some of those present will be thankful.

With those who have had contact with the Church the door is already open, and you may well, if you are a clergyman, have had some time to pray with the person who is now dead. It is a task which should not be left to the clergy to do, but the family can help as well and take on the opportunity to pray, if possible with the sick person. The trouble is we may feel it is embarrassing and really the job of the vicar, but this of course is not so. All it takes is a little courage and time. Use familiar prayers which you will have heard together in church. Even if the sick person cannot respond, remember that the hearing is the last thing to go, and the familiar prayers may well have a calming effect. Be simple and talk direct – if making your own prayers, always remembering to give thanks for the life that has been lived and the gifts which have been used in that life in so many ways. Always acknowledge the mystery of God's activity, and help each other see that even death is a part of it, the ongoing creation which is all a part of God's being.

It does take great sensitivity, especially if the person is not really aware that they are dying, but so often we are playing cat and mouse over this one. The sick person does not think that those who tend them know that they are dying, and the well people think that the sick person does not know that they are dying, and so neither side faces the facts, and so much good time is lost. There are ways of opening up to the idea of death but it can never be right bluntly to tell the person they are dying. It is much better to test the idea with suggestions in prayers, and to give the opportunity for the sick person to raise the question. Then if they do, put the question back to them and ask them what they think.

On those few occasions when I have had the opportunity to pray with people who know they are dying it has been a rich and rewarding experience. All the masks that we put up in life gradually fall away, and we can see things as they really are. I have been told by people at this stage of their existence that after the initial anger, fear and distress at the though of leaving those they love, there has come upon them a calm, and for the first time they feel a real person. If we think about this we can understand why. No longer do we have to pretend to be what we are not, as there is not going to be a long period before we leave this world. There is going to be a freedom from earthly worries like bills and taxes and how to pay the mortgage, and there is now time to reveal yourself and perhaps to discover things about yourself you did not know. In fact I have seen people positively blossom at this time in their lives, and their prayers have been full of thankfulness.

Not all people are as lucky as to know when they are dying, and indeed some may not be able to cope with the thought. The hospice movement has brought a great deal of reality to death and dying, and many people have been prayerfully helped through this stage of their lives by the staff of these places. I have often found that when praying with people who are dying there has been a great freedom, honesty and joy. If only we can face the challenge of sharing the prayers of the dying then I am sure we shall receive more than we can possibly give. In keeping our prayers open and simple and honest, we acknowledge that there is much we do not know as well, and we ask questions for the future.

11

The Words of Prayer

When reading *Honest to God* I felt at times
exhilarated, although not confessing to understand
all the points. What I did discover was that the writer
was putting into words my feelings and thoughts,
and articulating them for me. The prayers of the
Church can do as much for our prayer life. When we
are sterile they can often bring abundant riches to
release us and let us pray.

Like many churchgoers "Hymns Ancient and
Modern", and the prayers of the 1662 Prayer Book,
have influenced and coloured my spirituality. It may
be that the repetitive use of favourite hymns, or
vicars and organists have perhaps influenced us more
than the actual preaching from the pulpit, for those
words once heard are seldom put into print, and we
cannot remember them, whereas prayers and hymns
repeated time and again instil their meaning in us. If
I were to be asked my favourite hymn of all time it is
"Dear Lord and father of Mankind forgive our
foolish ways". It is more difficult to limit the choice
of prayers.

Have you often wondered what is being said by
members of congregations in those quiet moments at
the beginning and end of a service when they are
waiting for it to start, and the priest has returned to
the vestry and everyone is kneeling in silence? Has it

ever been suggested to you how best to use this time of preparation?

I offer here a simple choice of prayers which have helped me over the years. They may speak to each of us in different ways. For me they are prayers which have helped focus my attention and prepare my mind for a deeper understanding of all that attention we pay to God.

First we turn to a prayer which we can say quietly before we come to Communion. It is a prayer of St Thomas Aquinas.

> Almighty, everlasting God, lo, I draw nigh to the sacrament of Thine only-begotten Son, our Lord Jesus Christ. I draw nigh as one sick, to the Physician of life; unclean to the Fountain of mercy; blind, to the light of eternal brightness; poor and needy, to the Lord of heaven and earth. I implore, therefore, the abundance of Thine exceeding bounty, that Thou wouldest vouchsafe to heal my sickness, to wash my defilements, to enlighten my blindness, to enrich my poverty, and to clothe my nakedness; the Bread of Angels, the King of kings, and Lord of lords, with such reverence and humility, such contrition and devotion, such purity and faith, and with such purpose and intention, as shall be expedient for the health of my soul.

Grant me, I beseech Thee, that I may receive not only the Sacrament of the Body and Blood of the Lord, but also the substance and virtue of the Sacrament. O most merciful God, grant me so to receive the body of Thine only-begotten Son our Lord Jesus Christ, which He took of the Virgin Mary, that I may be worthy to be incorporated into His mystical Body and accounted among His members. O most loving Father, grant me, that Thy beloved Son, whom I now purpose to receive veiled from sight, I may at length behold for ever face to face. Who with thee, in the unity of the Holy Spirit, liveth and reigneth God, world without end. Amen.

This is not a short prayer. Its use before the Communion Service, said in a quiet place in the church or at home, does put into focus what we are about. I find that I am prevented from filling my mind with all other intentions when I use this prayer, and it prepares me to set calmly about the immediate taak of concentrating on the Communion Service.

The end of the service also offers us space for a "signing off prayer". Like the prayer above, I found the following in a Benedictine Monastic Diurnal or Prayer Book. It is an offering of our entire self to God after receiving the Sacrament.

Accept, O Lord, my entire liberty, my memory, my understanding, and my will. All that I am and have Thou hast given me; and I give all back to Thee to be disposed of according to Thy good pleasure. Give me only the comfort of Thy presence and the joy of Thy love; with these I shall be more than rich and shall desire nothing more.

A shorter and in some ways simpler prayer, reminding us of our dependence upon God and offering to live our lives for Him.

From my childhood days – and it must be fairly obvious to anyone who has read thus far that unsatisfactory as they now seem the influence of those who tried to instruct me in my most formative years still lingers – I remember by heart, as that is the way we were taught to learn, this prayer of St Ignatius Loyola.

Teach us, good Lord, to serve Thee as Thou deservest; to give and not to count the cost; to fight and not to heed the wounds; to toil and not to seek for rest; to labour and not to ask for any reward, save that of knowing that we do Thy will; through Jesus Christ our Lord.

I am sure that the Headmistress tried to instil this

prayer in us to create active minds and a good work ethic, for sure enough there was little or no reward other than a red star on your book for some really good efforts. It does as a prayer reflect our desire to discern the will of God for us, and so we ask for help in doing so, offering all our efforts to Him.

St Francis of Assisi has given us one of the most popular prayers when we come to pray for the needs of the world. This version is an adaptation from a book of Parish Prayers by Frank Colquhoun.

> Eternal God, the Father of all mankind: We commit to Thee the needs of the entire world. Where there is hatred, give love; where there is injury, grant pardon; where there is distrust, restore faith; where there is sorrow, renew hope; where there is darkness, let there be light; through Jesus Christ our Saviour and Redeemer.

The use of such a prayer before we add our own petitions to God for any needs that we see and wish to pray about, helps open our minds to the huge needs there are in the world and sometimes puts things in perspective.

My final prayer is one I learnt as a curate in Sherborne in Dorset. Once a week we were charged with the duty of taking prayer in the ancient Almshouse of St John the Evangelist at the gate of the Abbey close. The Chapel there is quite beautiful and still. It is a prayer which is used at the end of the service near the end of the day, and is the one I wish to end on. It is an adaptation of a prayer by Cardinal Newman.

> O Lord, support us all the day long of this troublous life, until the shades lengthen, and the evening comes, and the busy world is hushed, the fever of life is over, and our work is done. Then, Lord, in your mercy, grant us safe lodging, a holy rest, and peace at the last; through Jesus Christ our Lord.

If I were to have a prayer on my lips when I die then I would wish it to be this one. For some of us life is feverish and we do not find much peace, except tantalising glimpses which encourage us in our quest. We struggle to discern what God's will for us is, and how best we can use our talents in His service and for the good of our fellow men. The great thing is that no matter how inarticulate our prayers are, God hears and receives them. We may never see the success or otherwise of them but we have to work for the faith to go on.

*   *   *

Prayer is for all, there is no blueprint for survival, but many guidelines have been given us over the centuries. If you have on your shelf a book of prayers I hope you will reach for it and have the courage to use it. Look again at the prayer books we use in church, and read those familiar prayers again to yourself, quietly looking for ways that they speak to you. Above all, spend time on your own prayers and offer them to God.